THE MYSTERY OF INIQUITY REVEALED

Exposing the Unseen Spiritual Cancer
and Root Cause of
What is Destroying the Human Being,
the Church and the World Today

Julio Alvarado Jr.

The Mystery of Iniquity Revealed:

Exposing the Unseen Spiritual Cancer and Root Cause of What Is Destroying the Human Being, the Church and the World Today

Copyright © 2012

Julio Alvarado Jr. Publishing

ISBN 978-0-615-72491-1

Library of Congress Control Number: 2012923949

ALL RIGHTS RESERVED

No portion of this publication may be reproduced, stored in any electronic system, or transmitted in any form or by any means, electronic, mechanical, photocopy, recording, or otherwise, without written permission from the author. Brief quotations may be used in literary reviews.

Cover art by: Roland Ali Pantin

All Scripture quotations are taken from the Modern King James Version of the Bible, unless otherwise noted.

For information, please contact:

julio@julioalvaradojr.com

Endorsements

From the moment that Adam and Eve, my first human creations, ate the forbidden fruit from the tree of knowledge of good and evil, humanity has continued to eat of its fruit unconsciously. This tragic moment in history was birthed into the world through the strategic deception of iniquity, of which the serpent of old, your adversary, conceived and designed.

I have created you with a unique and wonderful purpose, one that Satan strategically attempts to conceal from you every day. His greatest tactic is revealed in the pages that follow.

The truth you will discover will empower you to recognize, develop and deploy the Kingdom that I have embedded within the DNA of your inner being, which is made according to the original image and likeness of who I AM and whom I have designed and purposed you to be.

I have commissioned my son Julio to write this book. I have instructed him to be transparent with his past and his present process of recovery. This book, although it has been a great blessing to Julio, is not exclusive to his life.

The content of this book applies to every human . . . to *you*.

Within the pages of this book you will find true and lasting answers to problems you have faced all your life.

You will discover why My voice is not being heard by those who claim to know me, and not being followed by those who claim to live for Me.

You will find the reason why there are so many beliefs and doctrines when I have only created one.

You will find the reason that the world as a whole is in the condition that it is in, and yet you will find hope that you have the power to be the change you want to see in the world.

If you seek Me with your whole heart as you read, you will find a spotless purity and an all-encompassing love, where iniquity has no place. You will find the power to free yourself from the entanglements of iniquity.

As you grow through this process, you will find that I have given you access to another tree: the Tree of Life. Its fruit will cause you to grow into whom I have purposed you to be before I even created the foundations of the world.

I will show you who **YOU** are **TRUTHFULLY** supposed to be ... and most of all, I will show you who **I** really **AM**.

God - The Creator

This book is timely, informative and has the power of deliverance that leads to true freedom for all of us who are struggling with inherited defective genes. The embarrassment of our favorite leaders and religious mentors are displayed in the media, swallowing up the last of our hope. Like we might do when we hear an ambulance wailing through our congested streets, when we hear of our fallen leaders day after day, we shudder to ask who may be next. God heard our cry and responded with true hope for all of humanity through this life-changing resource.

My good friend and colleague, Julio, felt the agony of the heart of men and woman around the world breathlessly crying out for help. He carefully penned this manuscript with the simplicity of transferring information that somehow never reached us in the early days of our lives. He boldly describes, unfolds, and exposes this unseen raging spiritual carcinogen and genetic deformity called iniquity. This cancer has paralyzed and eaten away at the roots of so many good people in the church, as well as world leaders, but it has finally met its match.

We can now rise up from the drowning sea of hopelessness and breathe again from the philosophy and ideology of the greatest teacher, the Holy Spirit, as He has inspired Julio to write this chronicle of hope. The author uses Bible characters to show how each one of them overcame their weaknesses and learned to live above their iniquity. Let the sound of Heaven resonate from each page of this book as it re-engineers our genetics and rewrites the equation of our true being again in the fabric of our DNA.

Thank you, Julio Alvarado, for listening to the voice of God and refreshing the earth with hope again. The Kingdom has truly come to earth through your obedience to the ultimate Creator and Sustainer of everything.

R. Pepe Ramnath, PhD
Research Scientist/Author/Pastor MCCI, FL

When you want to destroy a tree, the focus must always be on the destruction of the root, not the fruit. Since the horrific atrocity committed at the base of "The tree of the knowledge of good and evil," the world at large has been guilty of dealing the continual multiplication of spiritual and social ills. Due to the deceptive veil of iniquity we have unconsciously lost sight of "The tree of life," whose fruit holds the answers towards a complete exposure that leads to a renunciation of all traces of iniquity.

This book systematically reveals the unseen reason of all forms of misconduct that are present in the world today. Julio has illustrated a step-by-step process on how to discover and destroy "the diabolical root of iniquity" that up until now was an unknown enemy to the world today.

Finally the mystery of iniquity has been revealed! Read this book and see for yourself.

Benson Agbortogo
Chief of Mission
Kingdom Embassy Network

This book is easy to read and understand, providing an intrinsic look into the fundamentals of iniquity. A "must read" book, applicable for life changing and mind renewal. It is packed with sound Biblical references and Kingdom theology. I am pleased to recommend this book as a college text book not only for our Bible College, but also, any Bible College looking for sound text material.

Dr Roderick Howell
KME Institute, Chancellor
Freedom Bible College & Seminary, No. AL Branch Pres.

This groundbreaking treatise sheds extensive revelatory light on the topic of iniquity. Julio's research is delivered with such fiery passion not often found. The effect of iniquity on purpose is of particular interest to me. You can't afford not to read this life-changing book more than once. In addition, I would suggest you invite Julio to conduct meetings to expound further on this all-important topic of iniquity.

G. Alfred Palmer
CEO PurposeQuest International
Author of *Purpose-ology: The Science of Purpose*

Excellent book for spiritual increase and maturity! The signature of the author's heart is evident in each page and will make you discover an untapped reality in this world. It will draw you closer to understanding the truth of who you are.

Maria Nancy Bocalan Schwartz
Founder of Thy Kingdom Carriers, Inc.

Let freedom ring! Finally, a book that unlocks and confronts past, present and tomorrow. If you want answers to overcoming stumbling blocks, failures, and diseases that seem to "run in the family," I'd suggest you read this book. Julio exposes the "secret" that may be hindering all successes in your life and family. Reading through the pages was definitely an eye opening experience which caused me to retrace my bloodline seeking to eradicate strongholds, impediments and repeated cycles that ultimately are the result of the root cause of "iniquity" that has plagued many generations.

Definitely written for the 21st Century.

La Vada D. Humphrey
Kingdom Coach, Radio Personality, and Author

This Book Is Dedicated to:

Everyone who believes that there is more to them than what they are now and more to life than what they are currently experiencing.

Everyone who has an addiction but just can't seem to overcome it completely—whether it be food, drugs, alcohol, pornography or any other life-crippling habit.

Everyone who doesn't just want to be temporarily delivered from a stronghold in their lives but wants to be completely set free from it.

Everyone who has wondered if they really are unique individuals, purposed by God.

Everyone who has never been told, "I believe that you have the power to grow and change," but instead informed in a negative sense that they would always be like their father, mother or someone else.

Everyone born into a "dysfunctional family" where genuine love was not demonstrated due to abuse or the absence of proper parenting.

Everyone who wishes that they were never born.

Everyone who wishes that their family tree could be different and wants to change its fruit.

Everyone who knows they have a specific purpose in life but senses something blocking it from being discovered.

Everyone who wants to experience life to the full.

Everyone who is tired of corruption in leaders, either elected or those who take power by force.

Everyone who has ever wondered why we have so many religions, denominations and beliefs, with each one claiming to be right.

Every church or world leader who wants to bring true, positive change to the people they serve.

Everyone who struggles with hearing the voice of God.

Everyone who desires to discover the true Kingdom of God experience that they read about in their Bibles.

Contents

Endorsements i
This Book Is Dedicated to: vii
Foreword xiii
Acknowledgements xv
Introduction xix
    Across the World xx
    Within the Church xxi
    In Whose Image? xxii
    How to Use this Book xxiv

1. **What is Iniquity?** 1
       True Definition of "Iniquity" 3
       The Abuse of Truth 7
       Girded with Truth 8

2. **Where Did Iniquity Originate?** 13
       Iniquity's Influence in the Heavenly Realm 15
       Satan's Effect on the Earth 16
       Iniquity's Effect on Identity and Occupation 18
       King David's Inspired Insights 19

3. **Sin? Or Iniquity?** 25
       Definition of Sin 26
       A Clear Distinction 27
       The Mystery of Iniquity 28

4. **The Disciples, The Apostles and Iniquity**................33
   Knowledge without Wisdom 36
   Grace and Truth 38
   Kingdom of Heaven Hearing......................................40
   DNA — "Dynamic Named Ability" 42
   Manifesting His Name 44

5. **The Biology and Science of Iniquity**.......................49
   Iniquity of the Fathers 49
   The Firstborn... 52
   Biology or Iniquity? 54

6. **Iniquity of the Fathers Transferred** 63
   Raise up a Child... 64
   A Primary Responsibility... 67
   A "Real Man".. 69
   The Need for Spiritual Fathers 73

7. **The Iniquities of You and Me** 77
   Generations of Iniquity.. 78
   The Power of Truth 81
   Going by the Book... 82
   The Five Start Days 85
   Carrying the Cross 91

8. **Iniquity and the Church** 97
   What is the Church? 99
   The Importance of Strategic and Vigilant Prayer.... 104
   What is Faith?.. 108
   Purposed? 112
   According to the Will of God................................... 114
   The Importance of Vision to the Congregation 117
   The "God" Kind of Love.. 121

9. **Iniquity within the Family Unit**............................ 127
   Creating and Comforting 129
   Meant to be Courageous 131
   Beware of Judgment 135
   His Perfect Plan..136

10. Iniquity and the World 141
- The Root Reason 141
- The Olive Mountain Prophecy 142
- Signs of Iniquity Today 146
- City on a Hill 147

11. Jesus and Iniquity 153
- The Spotless Lamb 153
- The Straight and Narrow Way 154
- Grace and Truth Revisited 156
- Spirit and Truth 159
- Gospel of the Kingdom 162

12. Iniquity and the Kingdom of Heaven 171
- The Grip of Iniquity 172
- What Manner of Man is This? 173
- If You Love Me… 174
- Tale of a Talent 176
- The Great Symphony 178

13. The Blood, the Water and the Spirit 183
- Old Testament Remedy for Iniquity 184
- Three Essential Elements 187
- The Blood 189
- The Spirit of Truth 192
- The Water 193

14. The Iniquity Removal Process 197
- New Testament Confusion 198
- Grace Revisited – Grace that Saves 199
- Your Blood Type 203
- Our Fitness Trainer 205
- A Fresh Perspective on the Word "Scripture" 207
- The Fear of the Lord 209
- Quiet Time 212
- The Power of Fasting 214
- In Living Color 216
- Holy, Pure and Perfect 218

Conclusion 225

About the Author 229

Appendix: Definitions...231

Bibliography..239

Foreword

This erudite, eloquent, and immensely thought-provoking work gets to the heart of one of the most important and yet gravely misunderstood subjects in life – Iniquity.

This is indispensable reading for anyone who wants to understand and live life at the level God intended. This is a profound authoritative work by Julio Alvarado spans the wisdom of the ages and yet breaks new ground in its approach to understanding the concept and meaning of Iniquity and will possibly become a classic in this and the next generation.

This exceptional work by Julio is one of the most profound, practical, principle-centered approaches to the subject on Sin and Iniquity I have read in a long time. The author's approach to this timely and critical issue brings a fresh breath of air to a very mysterious subject and it captivates the heart, engages the mind and inspires the spirit of the reader.

The author's ability to leap over complicated theological and metaphysical jargon and reduce complex theories to simple practical spiritual biblically based principles that the least among us can understand is amazing.

This work will challenge the intellectual while embracing the laymen as it dismantles the mysteries of this little taught subject. This book delivers the profound in simplicity.

Julio's approach awakens in the reader the need to take an introspective journey to determine their state of spiritual maturity. The Author's antidotes empower us to rise above any self-defeating, self-limiting factors in our life and to pursue a life of spiritual exploits.

The author also integrates into each chapter the time-tested precepts giving each principle a practical application to life making the entire process people-friendly. The Bible will come alive while reading this book and the Kingdom will become practical.

Every sentence of this book is pregnant with wisdom and I enjoyed the mind-expanding experience of this exciting book. I admonish you to plunge into this ocean of knowledge and watch your life change for the better as you uncover the mysteries of iniquity and experience the Highest level of Kingdom Living.

Dr. Myles Munroe

BFM International
ITWLA
Nassau Bahamas

Acknowledgements

This book is a project that has been influenced and enhanced by numerous people, but let me begin by extending thanks foremost to God Almighty, who extended mercy to a man who was at the end of his rope in many ways.

Lord, thank You for not just saving my life but bringing sanity to my mind, health to my body and wholeness and completeness to my spirit in the process.

Thank You, God, for showing me the Kingdom that lies within me, "The Real Me" that You have mandated me to discover, develop and deploy into the world. Thank You for showing me "The Real You," which has been the greatest discovery of my life.

A deeply heartfelt thank you to my beloved wife, Ivette. Thank you for taking a chance on marrying a man like me. I wouldn't be half the man I am if it were not for you. Thank you, my love, for forgiving me, being patient with me and loving me like no other human has.

A deep fatherly love and appreciation to my children, Amaris, Ashley and Valentino, for loving me through my mistakes and forgiving me for my failures as a father. Thank you for giving me another chance and blessing me with the daily honor of still being called your "dad."

I want to thank my mom, Delia Martinez, and my dad, Julio Alvarado Sr.—who passed away recently—for loving me and doing your best with what you had.

I would like to thank my Pastors from World Outreach and Bible Training Center, Ervin (Skip) and Melva Henderson, for being real shepherds to me and my family. Thank you for the phone call that conceived the topic of this book. You both believed in me and gave me opportunities to incubate my personal growth and development. Thank you for your patience, love and prayers. Thank you for your inspiring words of "Julio, you have got the goods," and "We trust you." These will always mean a lot to me.

I would also like to thank the fertile ground of World Outreach and Bible Training Center for adopting my family in February of 2009 with an acceptance and love that we had never experienced before.

A special thank you to "The League of Extraordinary Men," the men's ministry, for allowing me to teach many of the principles found in this book at "Man School" and for loving me through the process. Your placement in my life has ministered to me in volumes that I will forever be grateful for. You all are truly extraordinary.

A special thank you has to be extended to Tony Rogers, a bank of knowledge, who encouraged me to write this book and to birth its existence. Tony, you mentored me with resources, ideas, and sharing your heart. I will never forget the phone conversation that we had when I was on my way to teach on this topic and your words, "Julio, out of all the books that I've ever read, I've never heard about this like you are explaining it—you should write a book about it."

I want to thank and acknowledge Ryan Roberts, my first mentor, who taught me how to never settle for just a word from God but to always get the details of that word. I will always carry your Trinidadian "Yeah Mon" wherever I go.

To my second mentor, Dr. Myles Munroe. In my opinion, a man who is a voice used by God to the earth. Dr. Myles, thank you for instructing and fathering me through your resources and mentoring program which have moved me to pursue a life functioning as a "son of God" and not just an ordinary man. Your placement in my life helped to save my marriage, my relationship with my children, and strengthened my knowledge of and relationship with God.

Acknowledgements

I want to thank Dr. Caroline Leaf and Dr. Pepe Ramnath for their life work that has added to my understanding of how unique and detailed God created all of humanity to be.

I want to thank Jeff Benner for his life work and resources that have enlightened my understanding of the scriptures in such a way that has removed the boredom and ignorance I once had of the Bible.

I want to also thank my editor, Bonita Jewel, for her insights and skills. You have truly been a gem and a Godsend. You took all of my writing errors and converted them into a work of art, a picture that speaks a much-needed answer into the human being, the Church and the world today.

"Son of man, I have made you a watchman for the house of Israel; therefore hear a word from My mouth, and give them warning from Me: When I say to the wicked, 'You shall surely die,' and you give him no warning, nor speak to warn the wicked from his wicked way, to save his life, that same wicked man shall die in his iniquity; but his blood I will require at your hand. Yet, if you warn the wicked, and he does not turn from his wickedness, nor from his wicked way, he shall die in his iniquity; but you have delivered your soul."

"Again, when a righteous man turns from his righteousness and commits iniquity, and I lay a stumbling block before him, he shall die; because you did not give him warning, he shall die in his sin, and his righteousness which he has done shall not be remembered; but his blood I will require at your hand. 21 Nevertheless if you warn the righteous man that the righteous should not sin, and he does not sin, he shall surely live because he took warning; also you will have delivered your soul."

Ezekiel 3:17-21

Introduction

Everyone loves a good mystery. Mystery books have always been popular. Everyone knows the name "Sherlock Holmes" and there are countless series of mystery books—from children's stories to graphic novels.

The original author of mystery, however, is God. He has created the physical world as a reflection of the spiritual world, and many things that we see and feel are reflections of things that remain unseen. As much as humanity learns about science and discovers about the world around us, so much remains a mystery.

Yet God, the author of our lives, gives us clues and hints. He leads us on a journey of discovery, so that things that remain unseen will be understood through faith, spiritual growth and revelation. The mysteries of God are buried under many layers of truth.

One such mystery is iniquity, and how it affects the world today. Although there are hints and clues all around us, much of it remains hidden to many individuals, churches and world leaders today. The mystery of iniquity has, for centuries, been shrouded in the veils of flawed understanding. Unfortunately, the mystery of iniquity has been ignored, or redefined and neutered of its significance.

To expose the mystery of iniquity, many layers of preconceptions need to be challenged and exposed. Inaccurate presuppositions must also be peeled away.

To understand the mystery of iniquity, we have to challenge our own assumptions and thought patterns in search of the truth. If you can suspend your position long enough to take a fresh look, you will understand the mystery of iniquity with a clarity you never imagined possible.

Across the World

The world is changing at a rapid speed. An explosion in information, knowledge and technology over the past hundred and fifty years has brought unprecedented change in the dynamics of how people in the world live, think and operate. With so many opportunities for growth and knowledge, you would think that the world would be forming into a better place. Peace, prosperity and plenty should be on the up-rise; issues like crime, violence and poverty should be on the decline. However, for some mysterious reason, the opposite is occurring.

Violence is increasing. Wars and internal conflicts have reached unprecedented levels. Gang rivalry and inner-city violence are spreading beyond the borders that once kept their "operations" somewhat in check. Even children are taking up weapons against other children, and against their parents. The threat of nuclear war still exists worldwide; governments and leaders have no regard for the sanctity of life. Just reading the newspaper regularly could (and should) cause someone to ask, "What is going on in the world today?"

Leaders of nations are losing their power and even their lives. This is sometimes due to corruption; other times it is at the hands of a people who are simply tired of the current conditions and desire freedom from oppression. World leaders are scrambling to find answers within their own governments and in many cases are applying temporary fixes, yet the problems remain.

Many parts of the world are still undeveloped and their people are struggling to survive. Even though these lands often have a wealth of natural resources that have the potential to sustain and prosper the nation, these resources remain untapped. This is often due to the lack of true, unselfish leadership and a framework where all can contribute their ideas and intrinsic talents so that they can corporately reap the benefits of their collaborative efforts.

Precious metals, rare materials, and even common resources are being used in an unsustainable manner. The drug trade, alcohol use, and other substance abuses are growing worldwide. The poor and innocent are being exploited, mistreated, and cast aside.

The very foundation of the family structure is in jeopardy. Men, women and children today are suffering from the lack of understanding and functioning within the role of God's original design for them. Millions of men have become permanent members of the prison systems for a variety of reasons. Many men and women are choosing homosexual lifestyles. Governments are changing laws, unnaturally redefining the family structure to accommodate the voice of an outspoken minority.

The economic crisis is spreading like an epidemic, even in countries that used to be prosperous. Families are being forced to default to a perpetual mindset of worry because of difficulties they currently face and nothing to look forward to but an uncertain future. Starvation and widespread diseases are still a reality in many countries today.

Within the Church

The church has, in many cases, failed to be a picture of true, living Christianity. Priests, pastors and other church leaders have been found guilty of grave misconduct, unhealthy lifestyle choices, and the misappropriation of church finances. Adultery is a common occurrence amongst church leadership and congregants. The divorce rate in the church is no less than the national average.

Young people who grew up in the church are abandoning their faith at an alarming rate, with many of them choosing lifestyles that include drugs, alcohol, partying, and sexual deviation—just to name a few. There remains little to no evidence that they have received any spiritual and moral training, which should have given them the truth about such unhealthy lifestyles.

Today many denominations and beliefs congregate under the umbrella of "religion." All claim to have truth or the mind of God, yet their practices, character, disagreements and manmade traditions do not portray the essence of who God really is. Much of what is being taught today caters more to the side of **entertaining** believers instead of **training** believers and equipping them with knowledge on how to strengthen their spirits.

Churches today are mastering marketing techniques to bring the people in and give them basic Bible knowledge, yet so few Christians are given what they need to truly connect with God. This is evidenced in little to no real change in the lives of believers. They achieve a marginal level of deliverance from sinful behaviors and past lifestyles but are not truly and permanently set free from dysfunctional thinking and unhealthy tendencies. They unfortunately accept this limited existence and just cope with it.

Whether the problem exists in the human being, the church or in the world at large, there is one common thread evident in these environments. There is something keeping health, peace, wholeness and prosperity from being manifested. Similar to a computer containing a virus that contaminates data and hinders the computer from functioning at its full capacity—and sometimes causing it to not function at all—there seems to be a hidden virus that is hindering our ability to grow and prosper, personally and in society at large.

In Whose Image?

Every human being has been made in the image and likeness of God. Each one of us has, within our "circuitry," an original, preordained purpose. It could be called a unique destiny. Every person on earth has been called and chosen for a specific purpose and contains the exact "programming," or abilities, they need to fulfill that purpose.

Introduction

Every human being on the face of the earth today is designed by God to properly care for the earth and to exercise positive dominion over all negative circumstances we see around us. We are meant to protect and care for the earth's resources, including its most precious resource—people.

Yet members of the human race, for the most part, lack any true sense of direction. So few people have clarity of purpose; they lack a vision for their lives so they find themselves in a constant survival mode. The world and the church continue to fight the sad **fruit**—divorce, depression, oppression, pornography, murder, suicide, terrorism, greed, violence, and hunger—without accurately dealing with the **root** cause. This root remains unknown and hidden beneath the surface.

I have personally been exposed to a number of these issues, and I would venture to say that you probably have faced at least one of these in your life as well. I was raised in a dysfunctional family. In the past, I succumbed to drug and alcohol addiction, pornography, and homosexual prostitution. I have been affected by divorce, financial ruin and suicidal tendencies. I have family members who have suffered and continue to suffer from these same conditions and more. I have been exposed to the abuse of church leaders who, instead of helping me, hurt me due to their dominant leadership and their false portrayal of reverence and holiness.

If you have ever had the thought that, "There has to be more to life than what I am currently experiencing and more to me than what I have become," I want to tell you, emphatically, "Yes, there is more!"

Within the pages of this book, you will discover the root cause of all of these negative conditions. The contents of this book will pave the way to your discovering "The Real You" and "The Real God" who created you. He holds the solution to every problem you face. He has all the answers you need to be successful and prosperous in every facet of your life.

God needs you, because you have a unique purpose to fulfill in this world.

How to Use this Book

What you're about to read has the potential to change your life in unprecedented ways.

This book looks at "Iniquity" and exposes it in a way you have never seen before. You will come to grasp the meaning of iniquity at its origin and come to understand its many forms and nuances.

Though I have never personally seen an atom, it does not negate the fact that science has proven it is the building block of all ordinary matter that exists. In the same way, iniquity cannot be seen, but its existence is the foundational root of all that is wrong in the human being, the Church and the world today.

Iniquity had been secretly infecting and destroying me and adversely affecting those that I had influence over as a result; I was desperate to overcome iniquity in my life. I am living proof that, since applying the remedies to issues I personally faced, my life is much better today. My prayer is that you will find the same positive results in your own life. I believe that you will! God's Spirit will not fail to work miracles in the lives of any that are open to Him.

This is not a book about religion from a traditional or denominational perspective. However, you will read numerous passages of Bible scripture to validate the content of this book. Direct translations from the original Hebrew and Greek will be used to give you a clearer understanding of the topic. All information within this book has been well researched, as have been the key remedies to root out iniquity.

In no way is this book intended to speak negatively about any denomination or belief. This book is not purposed to **offend** anyone, but to **defend** them by helping them to discover and eliminate any form of iniquity in their lives.

Rather than filtering this information from a traditional, religious or denominational perspective, I suggest that you take this information before God Himself to hear what He says about how the topic pertains to your life.

The purpose of this book is to provide vital information to all people, yet I am aware that the spiritual life and experience of the readers will vary greatly. If some of the chapters or concepts are difficult to understand at first glance, I encourage you to exercise patience and take the time to study and review them repeatedly. After taking the time to study, reflect and pray, the contents herein will not only make sense, but hopefully begin to change your life as well.

It might be easy to reject or criticize the truth of iniquity, especially when one is comfortable with their traditional beliefs or current lifestyle. It will be a challenge to instead take the steps of allowing God's Spirit to work in your life to make you a new person. If you determine to make the effort, you will not regret your decision.

If you are a praying person, ask God to reveal to you the areas of your life that iniquity is affecting. Don't miss the summary after each chapter; take time to prayerfully apply the recommended applications. Highlight all portions of this book that pertain to you and take additional notes if necessary.

This book will give you insight in how you can do your part in being an answer to the problems of the world today rather than adding to them.

The information in this book will not just bring a degree of deliverance to your life but will set you completely free to discover and fulfill "The Real You."

I am happy to embark on this journey of discovery, growth and change with you!

⌘

Chapter 1

What Is Iniquity?

Nevertheless the foundation of God stands sure, having this seal: "The Lord knew those who are His" and, "Let everyone who names the name of Christ depart from iniquity" (2 Tim. 2:19, NKJV).

Before a life-changing experience at the age of 26, my life was a perfect example of iniquity and I didn't even know that the word existed. There were other words more familiar to me, such as recovering alcoholic, drug addict, and thief. I was also guilty of adultery and pornography, but I had never heard the word iniquity. Of course, I was attempting to overcome these debilitating habits. I had gone through several drug programs and self-help groups—such as Alcoholics Anonymous, Cocaine Anonymous and Narcotics Anonymous. These meetings were a part of my regular schedule. I had even admitted myself into the psychiatric ward of a mental health institution, which was followed by numerous counseling programs.

This season of my life had begun to manifest itself when I was 13 years old. My parents divorced at that crucial time of my life and I began to experiment with drugs. I started by stealing a cigarette from my mother. After cigarettes, I began experimenting with marijuana, valium, alcohol, cocaine and many other drugs. Cocaine soon became my drug of choice and ultimately became a god to me.

These choices fueled a life of crime and a "do whatever I got to do" mentality to support my habits. Starting at the age of 14, I found myself incarcerated numerous times in juvenile institutions.

In 1985, at the age of 21, I got married. This marriage, with my first wife, produced two children, yet it was filled with grave issues such as adultery, which eventually led to a divorce after four troubled years. During this time my life was also plagued with financial ruin and numerous other issues.

By the time I was 22, I was a convicted felon incarcerated for embezzling over six thousand dollars from my employer, as well as for drug possession and an illegal gun possession. This time in jail was followed by six years of probation.

My life changed on October 22, 1989. I became what is traditionally called a born-again believer through the invitation of a friend I had been incarcerated with. In Jesus, I found true hope and a clear path to recovery. Yet just being a "Christian" was not the solution to all my problems; I was soon to find my journey was only just beginning. Though now a born again believer in the Christian faith, I still relapsed a number of times during my first few years of Christianity.

I married Ivette in April of 1993, who came into the marriage with a daughter from her first marriage.

In February of 2006, after being married for 13 years and a born again Christian for over 16 years, I experienced a unique encounter with God. This moment revealed that although I was a "religious" man, I was deficient in many areas of my spiritual and personal life. I was an underachieving "son of God" and was not acting as a Godly husband or father. This revelation birthed within me a hunger for God. It changed the very direction of my life, making me desperate to seek God and pursue an accurate Kingdom of God mindset that at the time I was wholly unfamiliar with.

I wanted the truth. I needed to know who God predestined me to be, and how I could be equipped to fulfill my purpose. The ensuing discoveries I made completely transformed my life; I also came to realize my responsibility to help others discover this same truth—that learning the truth about iniquity and overcoming its presence in your life will help you discover "The Real You" and enable you to follow God's original personal growth and development plan, which is to "Build Your Life from the Inside Out."

I don't remember exactly when I first heard the word iniquity. Even though it is mentioned numerous times throughout the Bible, it is rarely talked about in the Church today. On the rare occasions that I heard the term during my early years as a born-again believer, iniquity was always defined as "sin."

But do "sin" and "iniquity" have the same definition?

Are they used interchangeably just to add variety to the Bible text?

A question arose in my mind, one that soon transformed into a search for truth: What is iniquity?

I was soon to discover that the answer to this question was not a mere definition; it was actually an answer to "the root cause of all that is wrong in the world." Iniquity is an issue that plagues the world today; it is a disease that, unless treated and cured, has the potential to render humanity, the Church and world governments ineffective, impotent and ultimately without life.

True Definition of "Iniquity"

The *traditional* perception of the word "iniquity" differs greatly from *true understanding*, which can be gained through studying the root definition.

In *Strong's Concordance*—a common resource used to interpret Bible scripture—we find that the word "iniquity" is used 262 times in the King James Version of the Bible; its plural form, "iniquities," is mentioned in 55 verses.

In the *Webster-Merriman Dictionary*, iniquity is defined as "a gross injustice, wickedness, a wicked act or thing or sin."

Depending on where the word is found in the Bible, you will notice "strokes" of this word, with some of the definitions from the Hebrew origin such as: "evil, make crooked, pervert or perverse, bent, in vain, trouble and false."

From the Greek origin you'll find iniquity defined as: "injustice, unrighteousness, wrong and moral wrongfulness." [See appendix for exact definitions.]

In another common study resource, *Brown-Driver-Briggs Hebrew Definitions Dictionary*, you will find definitions similar to the *Strong's Concordance*, as well as additional insights: "guilt, twist, distort, violent deeds of injustice, mischievous purpose, evil plan or consideration." [See appendix for exact definitions.]

Much of the Bible was originally written in Hebrew, to those who lived in a culture very different from our own. The Hebrew language is much more detailed than many languages, including English. For this reason, English is limited in properly interpreting original Hebrew writings, especially key words, the root of which must be properly understood.

An example is the word "love." Depending on where the word is used in the scriptures, it could have five different root meanings, all defining a different form of love. Having an original "Hebrew understanding" helps us have an accurate interpretation of what God originally intended when speaking through the written Word of the Bible.

Prior to the block letter Hebrew writing of today, Hebrew writings were communicated in the form of drawings of specific items. Depending on how these pictures were combined, the result would be a root understanding of what was being communicated. This form of communication is called Paleo Hebrew, which means "Ancient Hebrew." Writings of Paleo Hebrew have been found in many archeological discoveries, some dating back to over 4,000 years ago. The great historical finding of the ancient scrolls found in the Qumran caves of Israel in 1948—known as the Dead Sea Scrolls—contained scrolls that were written in Paleo Hebrew.

These pictures would be similar to ancient Egyptian picture writings (Hieroglyphics), also discovered on walls and artifacts in many archeological discoveries and sites.

Paleo Hebrew uses a total of 22 pictures. Some Hebrew Rabbinical schools today use "Word Wheels," which are teaching resources derived from Paleo Hebrew. These Word Wheels are used to teach original Hebrew understanding of Biblical scriptures and are believed to be the most accurate study tool available to obtain a deeper understanding of all original Hebraic words in the Bible.

Paleo Hebrew is the origin of some of our modern-day alphabet. In the Hebrew culture it is known as the *alef bet*, which are the names for the first and second letter, "A" and "B" of the Hebrew alphabet.

A lesser-known resource called *The Ancient Hebrew Lexicon of the Bible* is derived from Paleo Hebrew. In defining the word "iniquity," it has an additional definition of the Hebrew word *âven*, which is one of the primary root words for iniquity. The *Ancient Hebrew Lexicon of the Bible* gives a deeper understanding of the word *âven*, which puts all the definitions we have explored thus far into a clearer perspective.

The Ancient Hebrew Lexicon of the Bible uses "vigor" to describe the absence of iniquity and "vanity" to describe the absence of vigor:

Vigor: The use of the power within the belly (or loins) for reproduction or creative work.

Vanity: The use of the power within the loins for vain or other improper purposes.

(AHLB#: 1014-J (N))

Iniquity is therefore using the power within us for vain or improper purposes. In other words, iniquity and vigor cannot coexist; when vigor is gone from our lives, vanity is what remains.

Vigor is also defined as "strength, energy or power to produce." Vanity is defined as "the state of being empty of original contents or usefulness." Therefore, the absence of vigor will always result in the presence of vanity.

Vigor is the substance of what the Bible calls "truth." The truth of God gives strength, energy and power to reproduce or create according to God's design. The absence of truth causes vanity, which results in iniquity.

This discovery opened my eyes and birthed a hunger in my heart to gain a full understanding of iniquity. I knew it was important to find out whether or not it held implications or power to affect my life in any way. What I learned astounded me and scriptures, such as the following one, were suddenly illuminated in my heart and now made sense.

> *"This I say therefore, and testify in the Lord, that ye henceforth walk not as other Gentiles walk, in the vanity of their mind, having their understanding darkened, being alienated from the life of God through the ignorance that is in them, because of the blindness of their heart"* (Eph. 4:17-18, KJV).

The ignorance that causes blindness of the heart is the absence of true knowledge. When I studied the word "vanity" from this passage, it connected to the definitions from the *Ancient Hebrew Lexicon of the Bible*. The Greek definition for vanity in this verse, according to *Thayer's Greek Definitions*, is the word *mataiotes*, which is defined as "want of vigor" and "what is devoid of truth and appropriateness."

According to the *Greek to Hebrew Dictionary of Septuagint Words*, the word *mataiotes* is the Hebrew word *riq* which, according to *Strong's Concordance* and the *Ancient Hebrew Lexicon of the Bible*, is defined as "empty of contents, no purpose." [See Appendix.]

The "want of vigor" speaks to a lack of desire or the strength, energy or power needed to produce and create. Therefore, iniquity is an original purpose that has been emptied due to a lack of truth.

The Abuse of Truth

> *"You can bend it and twist it...You can misuse and abuse it... But even God cannot change Truth." – Michael Levy*

The biblical principle of "truth" has been misused and abused throughout church history, now more than ever. Many religions today have "cornered the market" on a particular doctrine or denominational concept and call it truth. However, this is not truth.

Truth is the language of Heaven. It is original information purposed to nurture or feed the covenant that God has with humanity.

Whenever God creates something, He creates it with a purpose and for His purposes. That includes you. Human beings are placed center stage, so to speak, on earth. As such, God has a unique and great purpose for humanity as a whole, and for each individual.

Everything that God has created carries within itself the potential to reproduce. Since God is the source of all truth, it is His responsibility to provide that truth to a human so that he or she can reproduce, or create, what He purposed them to do. When something God created fails to fulfill God's original intention, it becomes devoid or absent of its original truth. It is then susceptible to functions that He did not desire nor design. The result is iniquity.

> *"He is the Rock, his work is perfect: for all his ways are judgments: a God of truth and without iniquity, just and right is he"* (Deut. 32:4).

Instead of using the traditional definitions of iniquity with words such as transgression, wickedness, lawlessness or sin—which are only manifestations of iniquity—consider the following definition as a working description for the rest of this book. It encompasses every definition mentioned above, as well as others that are included in the appendix.

As you grow in understanding of this concept, this definition will begin to validate itself through your experiences, enlightening your understanding of what iniquity really is at its core.

Spiritual iniquity: To take the truth of God and use it for vain or other improper purposes rather than using it for its intended creative or reproductive work.

In a subsequent chapter, we will explore further aspects of the definition of "vigor" to gain an understanding of *physical* iniquity.

Girded with Truth

To more fully understand the original definition of iniquity, a clear explanation of the word "loins" is needed. The following scriptures give instructions about the "loins of the mind."

> *"Wherefore gird up the loins of your mind, be sober, and hope to the end for the grace that is to be brought unto you at the revelation of Jesus Christ" (1 Pet. 1:13).*

> *"Therefore stand, having your loins girded about with truth, and having on the breastplate of righteousness" (Eph. 6:14).*

To gird is defined as "to be prepared, to be fully alert, to remove any hindrance that limits or stops your progress." We are instructed to be "girded with truth."

What is God saying to us through these passages? For one, He is referring to the loins of the mind, not loins of the hip—which is an ancient skirt of clothing that you might see in certain resources that define the word "loins." The Greek and Hebrew definitions of "loins" in *Strong's Concordance* state:

G3751 *osphus*—internally the place of procreative power (physically and spiritually).

H2783 *châlâts*—in the sense of strength, the seat of vigor, the seat of emotions, the mind, the interior self, reins.

We can conclude that the loins of the mind are the areas of thinking that affect our progress in life. If we are not careful about what is driving the "loins of the mind," we might fail to experience the power of God's truth—knowing who we are in God, and even who He is. The contents of that truth lie deep within the soul, the core of the human being. The soul is a place of power and strength. It is the brain's decision-making center where knowledge enters, influencing every decision that we make. The soul is what the Bible calls the heart.

Truth is the only thing that causes the loins of our mind to function accurately; anything else will cause it to beat improperly.

Since God is a God of truth, this process of girding up the loins of our mind with truth is the only way to be graced with a complete, uncontaminated revelation of the desire that God has for every believer, according to the following scripture.

> *"And we know that all things work together for good to them that love God, to them who are the called according to his purpose. For whom he did foreknow,* **he also did predestinate to be conformed to the image of his Son***, that he might be the firstborn among many brethren" (Rom. 8:28-29).*

We are known and predestined by God for a unique and individual purpose. Following that purpose is choosing vigor over vanity and truth over iniquity. It is taking the power of truth that is within the loins of our minds and using it for its intended creative or reproductive work, creating His will on earth.

⌘

Chapter Summary:

- Vigor is the power of truth that God desires to deposit within the loins of the mind (the heart) for creative or reproductive purposes according to His will.

- Vanity is emptiness that results from either failing to use or neglecting altogether the power of truth and instead functioning in improper or unintended purposes.

- Iniquity is misapplied truth or the complete absence of truth.

- Spiritual iniquity is using power of truth within the loins of the mind for vain or improper purposes rather than using it for its intended creative or reproductive work.

- Truth is the language from Heaven that comes from the mouth of God.

Application:

1. Take time to reflect and pray about what word better describes the life you are living today: "vigor" or "vanity."

2. Consider the idea of truth as something that comes from the mouth of God. Do you believe that you are currently receiving this type of information from God Himself in order to reproduce and create God's purposes for your life? Take some time to reflect on what that may look like.

3. What was your understanding of the word iniquity before reading this chapter? Begin to carefully consider how it may be currently affecting your life.

Chapter 2

WHERE DID INIQUITY ORIGINATE?

"The secrecy of an ancient catastrophic mystery that is revealed assigns clear understanding to the covertness of its purpose and thus should no longer remain concealed." – Julio Alvarado Jr.

Everything that exists today had a beginning at some point in time. This includes iniquity. The beginning of iniquity can be discovered within a portion of scripture so profound that many have missed its depth.

What is commonly known as the "fall of man" happened in a place called the Garden of Eden. Many people believe this is where sin—which is a *manifestation* of iniquity—first began. This was the world-changing event in which Adam and Eve disobeyed God's original command to not eat the fruit from "the tree of the knowledge of good and evil" [See Gen. 2:16-17]. Though this was the beginning of sin *on earth*, it was not its birthplace. Before this event took place, another event occurred, one encompassing in its scope and devastating in its effects on the earth:

"You were perfect in your ways from the day that you were created, **until iniquity was found in you**" (Ez. 28:15).

These words were spoken to Lucifer, an angel created by God. Today, this "angel" is more commonly known as Satan, the devil, and other names such as the prince of Tyre, our adversary, the Serpent, the deceiver, the tempter, the liar, the enemy and many others. How did Satan digress from being Lucifer—a name that means light bearer, brightness or morning star—to one whom Jesus referred to as the "The father of lies"?

It is commonly believed that the angels in Heaven constantly worship God in some form [See Isa. 6:1-3; Rev. 4:8]. It is also believed that Lucifer led one of these forms of worship—primarily, musical worship—and that this was the primary reason why he was created by God. It would be safe to say that this was the God-ordained, original purpose for Lucifer's existence.

Much has been said about Lucifer's downfall from the favor of God and Heaven. Many state that it was because of pride or because he wanted to be like God that he rebelled and was cast out of Heaven. These are true, yet they were only *manifestations* of the original reason. Notice the above verse does not say it was "because of your pride," "arrogance," "sin," or any other negative attitude or behavior that his perfection was corrupted. His perfection was distorted "once iniquity was found in him."

He was guilty of distorting his original purpose, thereby making himself void of the original reason why he was created, the truth of what he had been destined to do within God's perfect plan. God is a God of truth and no iniquity is found in Him; whatever He creates in its original state is perfect. Therefore, Lucifer would not have been created with iniquity in him.

> "He is the Rock, **his work is perfect**: *for all his ways are judgment: a* **God of truth** *and* **without iniquity**, *just and right is he"* (Deut. 32:4, KJV).

The moment Lucifer began to believe something other than his original heavenly and righteous purpose, his thought life shifted out of its God-ordained order; iniquity originated and the process of rebellion began.

Just as faith is the substance of things believed and hoped for and is the power that activates the unseen world of Heaven, iniquity is the substance that produces a twisted thought life, causing another invisible power, which we call evil.

Properly defined, evil is anything that is out of the original will of God.

Iniquity's Influence in the Heavenly Realm

Lucifer's influence in the area of worship was persuasive enough to cause one-third of the angels to join him in his rebellion against God's original plan [See Rev. 12:4, 9]. When someone is infected with iniquity, they can potentially contaminate those under their authority and environment. As a result, many can be negatively affected and infected. We will revisit this fact in other chapters of this book.

Lucifer was created to fulfill a purpose. His original purpose and placement were operating according to God's design. He functioned perfectly until "iniquity was found in him."

> *"Son of man, lift up a lament over the king of Tyre, and say to him, So says the Lord Jehovah: You seal the measure, **full of wisdom and perfect in beauty**. You have been in Eden the garden of God; every precious stone was your covering, the ruby, topaz, and the diamond, the beryl, the onyx, and the jasper, the sapphire, the turquoise, and the emerald, and gold. The workmanship of your tambourines and of your flutes was prepared in you in the day that you were created. You were the anointed cherub that covers, and I had put you in the holy height of God where you were; you have walked up and down in the midst of the stones of fire" (Ez. 28:12-14).*

Lucifer had an anointing of wisdom, power and ability within his loins. He was perfectly equipped—internally and externally—to create and produce musical worship unto the Lord; this was his blessed responsibility. Yet, in desiring to become something he was not created nor predestined to be, he willfully aborted this original truth and purpose.

Lucifer seized the power that rested within the loins of his mind. He began to use it in vain, for inappropriate purposes. He therefore birthed iniquity.

Satan's Effect on the Earth

Everything God creates in its original state is always perfect. Earth was created in perfection; every creation upon the earth likewise had a perfect purpose and design. Satan, when he rebelled from God, was evicted from Heaven and from God's presence. He was cast to earth with those angels that followed him in rebellion. His "iniquitized"[1] presence negatively affected the earth, again emphasizing that when an individual is infected with iniquity, they will doubtless affect and infect their environment.

> "In the beginning God created the heavens and the earth. And the earth was **without form**, and **void**; and **darkness** was upon the face of the deep. And the Spirit of God moved upon the face of the waters" (Gen. 1:1-2).

Notice that God created both the heavens (the atmosphere above the earth, including space) and the earth, but that only the earth was "without form and void" with "darkness upon the face of the deep." This was not said about the heavens.

It is worthy to note that Heaven, the ultimate environment, is where the presence of God Himself resides. Even a hint of iniquity is not allowed in His presence as He is a God without iniquity [Deut. 32:4].

---

[1] Iniquitized is a word that I coined to define someone or something that is affected by iniquity.

These three conditions that were present on the earth validate the idea that Satan must have been present on earth after God originally created it, yet before the "fall of man."

Let's examine three conditions using *Strong's Concordance* from a Hebrew perspective.

H8418 Without form: tôhû - root (meaning to lie waste); figuratively a worthless thing; adverbially in vain; confusion, empty place, in vain, vanity, waste, wilderness.

H922 Void: bôhû - root (meaning to be empty); an undistinguishable ruin; emptiness.

H2822 Darkness: chôshek - the dark; figuratively misery, destruction, death, sorrow, wickedness, ignorance. [An absence of knowledge or revelation].[2]

Iniquity has devastating effects. We are told that "God is not the author of confusion" (1 Cor. 14:33). Iniquity causes confusion, which can lead to the improper formation of something, rendering it worthless due to the collapse of its original purpose. Iniquity will always produce a void, which changes the biological and spiritual shape of someone or something's original design. Only God's perfect purpose can fill that void; without it, undistinguishable ruin will occur.

Iniquity will always be infested with darkness, which is a Hebrew idiom for "ignorance"—defined as "an absence of knowledge or revelation." This darkness, or ignorance, results in misery, destruction and sorrow. It leads to the death of God's original intentions.

The earth itself was negatively affected by Satan's "iniquitized" presence, causing confusion and distorting the truth. Satan influenced the perfected creation that God had made by transforming the earth into an unproductive place of

---

[2] Strong, James. *Strong's Concordance of the Bible.* 1st Ed. Thomas Nelson. 1991.

undistinguishable ruin. Satan's ultimate, evil purpose is to keep every individual ignorant of who he or she truly is in God. He seeks to thwart and disguise the truth and knowledge of who individuals really are in Christ and what their purpose is. [More on this point in a subsequent chapter.]

In Hebrew thinking, *light* is illumination that comes as a result of knowledge. *Darkness* is ignorance, absence of knowledge or revelation. The difference between knowledge and ignorance is like the difference between day and night. Knowledge or revelation, when it concerns God, is always truth.

When God speaks, He always speaks truth. In the following passage, God said let there be light (truth and knowledge), which will expose and separate itself from darkness (ignorance). This passage could not possibly have been referring to the sun, moon and the stars, which are the sources of our natural light, since they were created on the *fourth* day and the following statement was on the *first* day of creation [See Gen. 1:14-19].

> "And God said, Let there be light. And there was light. And God saw the light that it was good. And God divided between the light and the darkness. And God called the light, Day. And He called the darkness, Night. And the evening and the morning were the first day" (Gen. 1:3-5).

Iniquity's Effect on Identity and Occupation

Lucifer's iniquity changed his own original identity, not just in name but also in occupation. Not only was his name changed, but his function as a created being also changed. His role in life morphed from bringing honor and glory to God to being an enemy of God and humanity.

God hates iniquity since it distorts and perverts what He originally created, making it susceptible to vanity, evil, unrighteousness, lies and the ultimate departure from its original purpose.

This also gives us a clue as to why we see God change names to more accurately state a person's original intended identity, such as Abram to Abraham (Gen. 17:5), Sarai to Sarah (Gen. 17:15), Jacob to Israel (Gen. 22:38), and Simon to Peter (Matt. 16:16-19, Mark 3:16) to name a few.

A major truth that many fail to understand or even believe is that the statement "you were perfect in all your ways from the day you were created" applies to every single person God has created. The concept that "God doesn't make junk" comes to mind. Every human on this earth was conceived in the mind of God before the foundations of the world even existed.

> "Blessed be the God and Father of our Lord Jesus Christ, who blessed us with every spiritual blessing in the heavenlies in Christ; according as **He chose us in Him before the foundation of the world**, that we should be holy and without blame before Him in love, having predestined us to the adoption of children by Jesus Christ to Himself, according to the good pleasure of His will" (Eph. 1:3-5).

King David's Inspired Insights

The famed King David, whom the Bible says was a man after God's own heart, distinguished between iniquity and sin.

> "Behold, I was shapen in iniquity; and in sin did my mother conceive me. Behold, thou desirest truth in the inward parts: and in the hidden part thou shalt make me to know wisdom" (Ps. 51:5-6, KJV).

Some believe that King David made the above statements because he may have been conceived in an unlawful way. Others believe that he was expressing the fact that we are all born into a sinful world. It doesn't matter whether one or both of these theories are true since God inspired him to write these crucial words to magnify the fact that God desires truth in our inward parts (our loins). This is a key to discovering iniquity in one's self and to remove it from one's life.

It doesn't matter how you came into this world. Whether you were "planned" or not, every conception is ordained by God, even those that are produced in a less-than-ideal manner. This truth shows that abortion is unlawful in God's eyes; it is one of the saddest results of iniquity, for it steals, kills and destroys a life that God not only allowed to happen but ordained for His purpose.

> "But as many as received him, to them gave the power to become the sons of God, even to them that believe on his name: Which were born, not of blood, **nor of the will of the flesh, nor of the will of man, but of God**" (John 1:12-13).

Lucifer was predestined with a purpose. Every human also is predestined with a purpose from God. Within the loins of the mind of every human being rests a perfect design, as well as the gifts, talents and potential that is needed for that person to fulfill their specific purpose according to the will of God:

> "For we are his workmanship, created in Christ Jesus unto good works, **which God hath before ordained that we should walk in them**" (Eph. 2:10).

> "And we know that in all things God works for the good of those who love him, who have been **called according to his purpose**. For those God foreknew he also **predestined** to be conformed to the image of his Son, that he might be the firstborn among many brothers and sisters. And those he predestined, he also called; those he called, he also justified; those he justified, he also glorified" (Rom. 8:28-30, NIV).

Jesus gives us two remarkable insights into Satan's "iniquitized" tactics and purpose. He also gives His remedy for this and lets us know His ultimate purpose.

*"The thief cometh not, but for **to steal**, and **to kill**, and **to destroy**: I am come that they might have life, and that they might have it more abundantly"* (John 10:10).

*"Why do you not know My speech? Because you cannot hear My Word. You are of the Devil as father, and the lusts of your father you will do. He was a murderer from the beginning, and **did not abide in the truth because there is no truth in him.** When he speaks a lie, he speaks of his own, **for he is a liar and the father of it.** And because **I tell you the truth**, you do not believe Me"* (John 8:43-45).

There are two spiritual fathers in this life:

> The Devil – the father of lies (John 8:44)
>
> God – the Father of truth (John 1:14)

One "father's" mission is to steal, kill and destroy your original identity and purpose in life through his hidden tactic of iniquity.

The other Father's mission is to reveal and develop your original identity and purpose through His remedy of Truth.

Once I personally discovered what iniquity was in its most basic form, I had to admit that the cancer of it was also in my heart. Until that point I had been living as a faithful, praying man for 20 years. I attended church two to four times a week. I taught Bible studies. I tithed and gave offerings. I performed many other religious activities. Yet none of that ultimately mattered because the Devil himself was fathering me through the bait and hook of iniquity and I didn't even know it.

The question that every human being has to ask is, "Who is fathering me?"

It is often a difficult question to ask. Yet the answer will determine your success and effectiveness as a Christian—or as I prefer to say, "A Kingdom of Heaven Citizen."

It will ultimately determine your ability to accomplish your God-given purpose and destiny.

⌘

Chapter Summary:

- Lucifer's fall from Heaven was the result of the iniquity that was found in him.

- Evil is anything that is out of the original will of God.

- Iniquity will eventually culminate in the failure to fulfill God's purpose and predestination for one's life.

- Iniquity distorts what God has originally created and ordained.

- **Spiritual iniquity:** Taking the power of truth within the loins of the mind and, rather than using it for its intended creative or reproductive work, using it for vain or other improper purposes.

APPLICATION:

1. Have you ever asked God about His unique plan and purpose for your life? If not, take some time to pray and reflect about it.

2. If you have asked or knew at one point, perhaps it is time to review that purpose and determine whether you are still following His plan for your life.

3. Looking at the concept of the two spiritual fathers mentioned in this chapter: the Devil – the father of lies and God – the Father of truth, who would you say is currently "fathering" you?

Chapter 3

Sin? Or Iniquity?

"Understanding the original definition of a key word, versus the assumption of its meaning, unlocks the intention and application of its purpose, which can determine it's life interpretation." – Julio Alvarado Jr.

As I mentioned earlier, iniquity was a word I rarely heard during more than 20 years of Christianity. When it was mentioned, iniquity was always defined as sin. However, these words are not interchangeable. Sin is not iniquity, but is *a result of* iniquity. Prior to becoming a believer, I don't recall ever hearing the word iniquity. The word sin was one that I heard fairly often though, even in some of the R-rated movies and music that I used to listen to.

When people of different religions would approach me on the streets or come to my door to share their beliefs, the topic of sin always came up. These people would often say, "Did you know that Jesus died for your sins?" or "If you died today, do you know that you will die in your sins?" Yet I don't recall any of them ever mentioning the word "iniquity."

Iniquity is not a word taught in the school systems that I attended as a youth. It is not a word that you will hear in casual conversation at home or on the streets. It is not a word used in the news or any type of entertainment television program. However, in all of those environments, the word "sin" is mentioned—at least occasionally. A majority of people have a basic understanding that sin is something wrong or evil that someone has done.

Since my discovery of iniquity's deeper meaning, and the insight that God has given me on its disabling grip in my life, the perception that "it's just sin" is no longer valid for me. Iniquity is not just something wrong that someone is doing. It goes deeper than that. Sin stems from iniquity—the failure to make decisions according to the creative purpose of God.

Definition of Sin

Iniquity and sin are two separate things. They don't have the same meaning.

The word sin is mentioned in approximately 389 verses in the King James Version of the Bible. Depending on the verse, you will find a variety of definitions. In *Strong's Concordance*, sin is defined as, "an offense, to miss the mark; harm done, guilt, cause of trespass, rebellion, and transgressions."

In the *Brown-Driver-Briggs Hebrew Definition Dictionary* you will find similarities to the *Strong's Concordance*, such as, "to miss the mark, incur guilt, offense, rebellion, transgression," as well as some more detailed definitions such as, "to miss the goal or path right and duty or wander from the way."

The *Ancient Hebrew Lexicon of the Bible* takes the definition to a deeper level: "a missing of a target, a sinner who misses the mark, and offender, one with faults or offenses, one with the character of wrongdoing, the wrong actions of one who is measured correct action, to revolt."

In *Thayer's Greek Definitions Dictionary*, sin is defined as, "to miss the mark, to err, be mistaken, to miss or wander from the path of uprightness and honor, to do or go wrong, to wander from the law of God, violate God's law, sin."

A common definition for sin, in all the above resources, is simply "to miss the mark." This definition is derived from the Hebraic concept of one who fails to hit the "bull's-eye" or core center of a target. God's will is considered to be the center of that target.

When you compare the definitions of iniquity and sin, you can see common threads, yet there are also major differences between the two words. Sin is a manifestation or result of iniquity because one cannot hit the center target of God's will without the pure and undefiled truth of God.

When we compare our working definition for iniquity with the common definition for the word sin, we can see a difference.

Iniquity: To take the power of truth within the loins of the mind and, rather than using it for its intended creative or reproductive work, to instead use it for vain or other improper purposes.

Sin: To miss the mark or target of God's original will for something.

Whenever the truth of God is unclear or perverted in our lives, we will fail to hit the mark or target of God's originally intended will. Therefore, sin is a result of iniquity.

A Clear Distinction

The scriptures make a clear distinction between "iniquity" and "sin" in approximately 50 verses from the King James Version of the Bible. Following are some examples:

> *"And he said, If now I have found grace in thy sight, O Lord, let my Lord, I pray thee, go among us; for it is a stiff necked people; and* **pardon our iniquity and our sin**, *and take us for thine inheritance" (Ex. 34:9).*

> *"I acknowledged* **my sin unto thee, and mine iniquity have I not hid**. *I said, I will confess my transgressions unto the LORD; and thou forgavest* **the iniquity of my sin**" *(Psalms 32:5).*

*"For I will declare **mine iniquity**; I will be sorry **for my sin**"* (Psalms 38:18).

*"It may be that the house of Judah will hear all the evil which I purpose to do unto them; that they may return every man from his evil way; **that I may forgive their iniquity and their sin**"* (Jer. 36:3).

*"But **your iniquities** have separated between you and your God, **and your sins** have hid his face from you, that he will not hear"* (Isa. 59:2).

*"For I will be merciful to their unrighteousness, and **their sins and their iniquities** will I remember no more"* (Heb. 8:12).

The Mystery of Iniquity

Many Christians today know what sin is, yet iniquity is still a mystery to them. The church often talks about sin, but rarely (and sometimes not at all) brings up the topic of iniquity. Due to a lack of education in the church on the subject of iniquity, many Christians today are not even aware of its existence. They are therefore unable to overcome it as they are ignorant of its consequences in their lives. This is why many believers today struggle with oppression, depression, marital problems and many other defeating obstacles in their lives. In spite of their faith in God and religious practices, many Christians intensely struggle with addictions, temptations and other spiritual afflictions. They do their best to deal with "sin" and often barely manage to control it when it manifests itself in their daily lives. Few understand that the root cause of sin is iniquity, which remains a mystery, even among Bible-believing Christians.

*"For the **mystery of iniquity** doth already work: only he who now letteth will let, until he be taken out of the way"* (2 Thess. 2:7, KJV).

In some translations of the Bible, "iniquity" and "sin" are defined as "lawlessness." In principle, lawlessness is a *result* of sin in that it is a violation of a law that God has established. Whenever God speaks—whether it is His voice speaking to someone's heart, or His written instruction in the Bible—He is in principle establishing a law. A Hebrew definition for law is "what creates order."

The words God speaks are "spirit and life." They will always create newness of life or purpose in some way. Any violation of an established word from God is breaking the law of God. In other words, it is lawlessness. Lawlessness is a result of iniquity because it violated a truth of God.

If you were to list what is wrong with the world today, you would most likely use words such as evil, greed, lustfulness, pride, stubbornness, selfishness, rebellion, disobedience, or your choice of many available terms. Each of those words has a distinct meaning and function, yet they all have their foundation in iniquity.

Lucifer's fall was the result of iniquity being found in him [Ez. 28:15]. This caused him to disregard the original purpose for his existence which led him to sin—to miss the mark. The act of ignoring his original purpose, instead choosing sin, was the birthplace of iniquity. Every negative characteristic we see in the world today—evil, disobedience, pride, rebelliousness, perversions, etc.—stem from his iniquitous nature and character.

⌘

Chapter Summary:

- Iniquity and sin do not share the same meaning.
- Sin is a result of iniquity.
- Iniquity is to use the power of truth for vain or other improper purposes, rather than using it for creative or reproductive work.
- Sin is to miss the mark or target of God's original will for something.

APPLICATION:

1. Write down how you would have defined "sin" and "iniquity" before reading this chapter.

2. Now write down your new definition of the words after having read this chapter. Are they greatly different?

3. Write down any thoughts you have on this new information.

Chapter 4

THE DISCIPLES, THE APOSTLES AND INIQUITY

"Until the day He was taken up having given directions to the apostles whom He chose, through the Holy Spirit; to whom He also presented Himself living after His sufferings by many infallible proofs, being seen by them through forty days, and speaking of the things pertaining to the Kingdom of God" (Acts 1:2-3).

The concept of iniquity is found throughout the Bible. Though it is primarily mentioned in the Old Testament, Jesus' disciples and the early apostles also wrote about iniquity.

After His resurrection, Jesus spent 40 days on earth teaching subjects pertaining to the Kingdom of God [Acts 1:3]. It is safe to surmise that He taught on the subject of iniquity, since it is mentioned at least 15 times in the New Testament after the four Gospels.[3]

Jesus only taught what He heard and saw from God the Father [John 5:19-20, 8:28]. His teaching on this crucial subject was therefore straight from Heaven. It's no wonder that the disciples and apostles carried on what they were taught by Jesus Himself and what the Holy Spirit inspired them to write and teach.

---

[3] A later chapter will visit Jesus' dealings with iniquity when He was on earth.

In Acts 1:16-18, Luke wrote of Judas' "reward" for his iniquity. He purchased a piece of land, now a cemetery, called "The field of blood." It is the place where he committed suicide by hanging himself once the weight of his betrayal—selling Jesus for 30 pieces of silver—was too much for him to bear [Matt. 26:14-16]. In a way, that act was prophetic; the iniquity in Judas' heart drove him to suicide—which is a common tragedy in the world today.

The cause for many suicides these days is rooted in iniquitized mindsets: oppression, depression and other negative, distorted and perverted thinking patterns that cause one to give up on life. The tragic and unnecessary act of suicide is the ultimate outcome of iniquity and letting go of the beautiful gift of life while forsaking the God-given destiny of a purpose-driven life.

In addition to physical suicide, there are also other forms of suicide—emotional, financial and spiritual. It is in essence, aborting God's will for one's life. In the following passage, Luke highlights the primary blessing that we received from God through His Son, Jesus. Along with the born-again life that He brings, He gives us the blueprint on how to turn away from iniquity.

> *"Unto you first God, having raised up his Son Jesus, sent him to bless you, in turning away every one of you from his iniquities"* (Acts 3:26, KJV).

The Apostle Paul, in 1 Corinthians Chapter three, addressed a problem that is still alive in the church today: the failure to teach the meat of the Word of God. For fear of offending someone, or not wanting to lose a congregation, many pastors today find themselves having to teach at a spiritual level of "milk" rather than "meat." Many believers desire to remain attached to worldly influences, which results in an immature relationship with God. The carnality of many believers causes them to walk after the ways of the flesh instead of following Christ's life-giving words, which includes His teaching on iniquity.

> *"And I, brothers, could not speak to you as to spiritual ones, but as to fleshly, as to babes in Christ. I have fed you with milk and not*

> with solid food, for you were not yet able to bear it; nor are you able even now. For you are yet carnal. For in that there is among you envyings and strife and divisions, are you not carnal, and do you not walk according to men? For while one says, I am of Paul; and another, I am of Apollos; are you not carnal? Who then is Paul, and who is Apollos, but ministers by whom you believed, even as the Lord gave to each?" (1 Cor. 3:1-5).

In this same chapter, Paul clues us into the major requirement necessary to overcome iniquity: the grace of God. Grace is traditionally defined as *unmerited or undeserved favor*. Grace is, in fact, God's provision and access to truth, which gives someone the ability to keep God's laws. I'm not talking about the letter of the law, or the written requirements, but the *spirit* of the law [Rom. 7:6], the principles behind the laws that have been given.

Paul was chosen by God to fulfill the role of an Apostle because of his expertise in the written law, or the letter of the law. His past, as an expert of the law, and his present, which encountered the presence of God, gave him a unique understanding of grace *through truth* [Rom. 7:6].

Paul's teachings were built upon the foundation of Jesus Christ. Paul gives a warning along with instruction on how to build our lives on top of the foundation of Jesus Christ.

> "According to the grace of God which is given to me, as a wise master builder, I have laid the foundation, and another builds on it. But let every man be careful how he builds on it. For any other foundation can no one lay than the one being laid, who is Jesus Christ" (1 Cor. 3:10-11).

The presence of iniquity will never accurately fit on the foundation of Christ. Iniquity is the wood, hay and stubble that will not pass the test of fire:

> "And if anyone builds on this foundation gold, silver, precious stones, wood, hay, stubble, each one's work shall be revealed. For the Day shall declare it, because it shall be revealed by fire; and the

fire shall try each one's work as to what kind it is. If anyone's work which he built remains, he shall receive a reward. If anyone's work shall be burned up, he shall suffer loss. But he shall be saved, yet so as by fire" (1 Cor. 3:12-15).

Knowledge without Wisdom

Iniquity births man's wisdom, which is contrary to the wisdom of God. Iniquity disguises man's and the world's wisdom as godly wisdom. Paul encourages believers to admit that we are fools because we often fail to apply truth-based knowledge, instruction and wisdom. In other words, Paul is saying be honest about where you are at and empty yourself of what you currently consider to be wisdom. Godly wisdom is knowledge that comes from the mouth of God. It then has to be understood and applied. This was the reason that Jesus was called "the wisdom of God" [Luke 11:49, 1 Cor. 1:24]. Anything less than this is our wisdom, which is usually worldly. As long as we cling to it, it will be impossible to obtain the true knowledge of God. If we want to manifest God's wisdom in our lives, we must understand and apply true knowledge from God.

> "Do you not know that you are a temple of God, and that the Spirit of God dwells in you? If anyone defiles the temple of God, God shall destroy him. For the temple of God is holy, which you are. Let no one deceive himself. If anyone among you seems to be wise in this world, let him become a fool so that he may be wise. For the wisdom of this world is foolishness with God; for it is written, 'He takes the wise in their own craftiness.' And again, 'The Lord knows the thoughts of the wise, that they are vain'" (1 Cor. 3:16-20).

Even before his conversion, Paul was a religious man whose name was Saul, taught by perhaps the best teachers of his day. Saul had authority from the chief priests to imprison and even put to death believers of Jesus Christ. It was on his journey to Damascus to fulfill this type of assignment that the iniquity-removal process in his life began [Acts 9:3-6, 22:6-10, 26:10-19]. This became the starting point for Paul to discover the preordained will of God for his life.

The lesson we can learn from Paul's experience is that as long as iniquity is present in our lives, we might have *knowledge* of God's Word but still not understand the *truth* of the Word. We can be blind to God's purpose for our lives and even be fooled into thinking that we are doing the right thing. Saul was a practitioner of iniquity; the one who was considered lawful in the eyes of man was actually practicing lawlessness in the eyes of God. It was Paul's discovery of the truth about himself, through the clear voice of Jesus, that paved the way for him to receive insight as to who he really was ... and who God really is. Paul's born-again experience birthed the real him.

Satan desires to steal, kill and destroy your identity. You must fight against his lies in your life and strive to let your identity line up with the manifestation of a son or daughter of God, obedient to the truth of who you are in Christ. Every born-again, spirit-filled believer has the potential to manifest his or her Godly identity [Rom. 8:13-17, 28-30 and 1 John 3:1-10].

When Jesus made comments like, "I tell you the truth..." or "I am the way, the truth, the life..." or "you shall know the truth and the truth shall make you free" (John 8:32, 45; 14:6), He was making statements that came from the original source of our lives: the Father. One of the main definitions for the word father is "source." God the Father is the only source authorized to tell us the truth of who we really are. After all, He was the One Who created us [Eph. 1:2-5]. Any other source—including ourselves—that we use to make up our own identity, even if we do so "in the name of Christ," is prone to the influence of another father—the father of lies, Satan.

Again, the question that we all must ask ourselves is, "Who is fathering me?"

When truth is not known or accepted, iniquity is present.

Paul's writings, inspired by the Holy Spirit, give us hope that we can be set free from iniquity. He informs us that the grace of God has appeared to all men in order to bring salvation. He also says that this same grace teaches us to deny any form of ungodliness and worldly lusts. He instructs us to live a righteous life so that we may have access to redemption from iniquity. We then become servants of righteousness. (We will explore the importance of righteousness in another chapter.)

> *"For the grace of God that brings salvation has appeared to all men, teaching us that having denied ungodliness and worldly lusts, we should live discreetly, righteously and godly, in this present world, looking for the blessed hope, and the appearance of the glory of our great God and Savior Jesus Christ, who gave Himself for us that He might **redeem us from all iniquity** and purify to Himself a special people, zealous of good works" (Titus 2:11-14).*

Grace and Truth

Though grace is a free gift of God [Eph. 2:8], its benefits come through the voice of truth, which we must obey to experience righteous living absent of the influence of iniquity. Jesus introduced grace and truth to the earth as a packaged benefit, not as separate components.

> *"... and the Word became flesh, and tabernacled among us. And we beheld His glory, the glory as of the only begotten of the Father, full of grace **and** truth" (John 1:14).*

> *"For the Law came through Moses, but grace **and** truth came through Jesus Christ" (John 1:17).*

Grace is the doorway to truth. God's grace enables His teaching to come alive in our lives through the Spirit of Truth: "For *the grace of God that brings* salvation has appeared to all men, *teaching us*" (Titus 2:11, 12). The Spirit of Truth is this teacher.

Many today confuse the *grace* of God with the *mercy* of God. God is merciful in that He provided grace and truth so that we can correct our "iniquitized" ways. It is impossible to live righteously without hearing, understanding and being obedient to the guidance of a righteous God. When God speaks to you, His instructions should act as your guiding light through the knowledge of truth [See 2 Tim. 3:15-17].

> *"That as sin hath reigned unto death,* **even so might grace reign through righteousness** *unto eternal life by Jesus Christ our Lord"* *(Rom. 5:21, KJV).*

Romans Chapter 6 outlines the cautions and implications of a false understanding of grace. Below I have included the entire chapter interspersed with other key verses. These passages bring a clearer understanding of the fact that grace is not a license to sin. Grace is the favor of God through the provision of truth. God gives us grace through truth to kill the carnal nature within ourselves so that we can walk in newness of life. This is the ultimate benefit of God's grace, which He desires for every human to take on as their transformed nature.

> *"What shall we say then?* **Shall we continue in sin, that grace may abound? God forbid.** *How shall we, that are dead to sin, live any longer therein? Know ye not, that so many of us as were baptized into Jesus Christ were baptized into his death? Therefore we are buried with him by baptism into death: that like as Christ was raised up from the dead by the glory of the Father, even so we also should walk in newness of life" (Rom. 6:1-4).*

Paul clearly tells us that God has granted us grace, yet this is not a license to continue sinning. Whenever we fail to hit the "bull's-eye" of God's will for our lives, we are guilty of missing the mark—sinning. The purpose of being "buried with Jesus Christ" is to produce the death of our own will so that we can walk in newness of life. This "baptism into death" should lead every believer to a place where they can clearly hear the voice of the Holy Spirit daily.

We are then, in essence, dead to our own will, and only then are we truly alive in the spirit.

Kingdom of Heaven Hearing

The following passages give us insight into how this process works. If understood and applied, this will result in what I call "Kingdom of God thinking that comes from Kingdom of Heaven hearing."

> *"If then you were raised with Christ, **seek those things which are above**, where Christ is sitting at the right hand of God. **Be mindful of things above, not on things on the earth**. For you died, and your life has been hidden with Christ in God. When Christ our Life is revealed, then you also will be revealed with Him in glory. Therefore put to death your members which are on the earth" (Col. 3:1-5).*

The only way to be "mindful of things above" is to listen to the voice that comes from above. Iniquity-free, Kingdom-of-Heaven instructions will always produce a person that is dead to their own will, which will lead to the discovery of the Kingdom of God within themselves. This will produce someone that is clothed in Christ alive. Iniquity caters to the carnal nature, hindering the fullness of Christ from being manifested.

> *"For **if** we have been planted together in the likeness of his death, **we shall be also** in the likeness of his resurrection: Knowing this, that our old man is crucified with him, that the body of sin might be destroyed, **that henceforth we should not serve sin. For he that is dead is freed from sin"** (Rom. 6: 5-7, KJV).*

To be planted together in the likeness of Jesus' death requires you to daily "carry your cross," symbolic of daily ensuring that *your* will—with its passions and desires—is crucified [Gal. 5:24]. This is a requirement to following Christ. Iniquity will always cause you to loosen the grip of the cross. It is impossible to completely lose your life for the sake of God if iniquity is present.

> *"And he said to them all, if any man will come after me, let him deny himself, and take up his cross daily, and follow me. For whosoever will save his life shall lose it: but whosoever will lose his life for my sake, the same shall save it" (Luke 9:23-24).*

Just because God has manifested His love towards us through the divine gifts of mercy and grace, we must not be deceived in thinking that grace is an automatic ticket to the daily benefits and eternal reward of Heaven.

> *"Now if we be dead with Christ, we believe that we shall also live with him: Knowing that Christ being raised from the dead dieth no more; death hath no more dominion over him. For in that he died, he died unto sin once: but in that he liveth, he liveth unto God.*
>
> *"Likewise reckon ye also yourselves to be dead indeed unto sin, but alive unto God through Jesus Christ our Lord. Let not sin therefore reign in your mortal body, that ye should obey it in the lusts thereof.*
>
> *"Neither yield ye your members as instruments of unrighteousness unto sin: but yield yourselves unto God, as those that are alive from the dead, and your members as instruments of righteousness unto God. For sin shall not have dominion over you: for ye are not under the law, but under grace.*
>
> *"What then? Shall we sin, because we are not under the law, but under grace? God forbid. Know ye not, that to whom ye yield yourselves servants to obey, his servants ye are to whom ye obey; whether of sin unto death, or of obedience unto righteousness?*
>
> *"But God be thanked,* **that ye were the servants of sin**, *but ye have obeyed from the heart that form of doctrine which was delivered you"* [See Deut. 32:1-5 to see the origin of the doctrine].[4]

---

[4] This "form of doctrine" is truth that comes from the mouth of God.

*"**Being then made free from sin, ye became the servants of righteousness.** I speak after the manner of men because of the infirmity (weakness) of your flesh: for as ye have yielded your members servants to uncleanness and **to iniquity unto iniquity;** even so now **yield your members servants to righteousness unto holiness. For when ye were the servants of sin, ye were free from righteousness.**

"What fruit had ye then in those things whereof ye are now ashamed? For the end of those things is death. But now being made free from sin, and become servants to God, **ye have your fruit unto holiness,** and the end everlasting life. For the wages of sin is death; but the gift of God is eternal life **through Jesus Christ our Lord"** (Rom. 6:8-23, KJV).

DNA — "Dynamic Named Ability"

Paul, in his second letter to Timothy, stressed the importance of removing iniquity if we are to identify with Christ.

"Nevertheless the foundation of God stands sure, having this seal: 'The Lord knew those who are His.' And, **'Let everyone who names the name of Christ depart from iniquity'"** (2 Tim. 2:19).

A foundational importance of the severity of what Paul was inspired to write can be traced back to the original Ten Commandments, which we are still supposed to honor. The third commandment inscribed by the finger of God states:

"Thou shalt not take the name of the LORD thy God in vain; for the LORD will not hold him guiltless that taketh his name in vain" (Ex. 20:7 and Deut. 5:11, KJV).

Many teach that the third commandment is saying we should not use any form of the name of God in a disrespectful way, such as cussing. Though this should not be done, it is not what this commandment is truly teaching.

"Vain" is the root word for "vanity," which is one of the primary words derived from "iniquity." To take the name of the Lord in vain means to take God's original identity for your life and turn it into a state of vanity: "being empty of the original useful contents and purpose through perversion or twisted actions, making it worthless and devoid of truth."[5] A believer who rightfully applies the name of God upon their life will create and reproduce all that the Holy Spirit tells and shows them.

God's voice and vision comes to us through the inner senses of the spirit: the inner eyes and inner ears. Our brain contains both the conscious mind and the subconscious mind, which the Bible calls the heart—the power center of our choices. This is the place that Jesus, our greatest example on earth, reproduced and created all that we know. We have access to the same DNA (Dynamic Named Ability) through the Holy Spirit. This revelation amazes me.

> *"Howbeit when he, the Spirit of Truth, is come, he will guide you **into all truth**: for he shall not speak of himself; but whatsoever he shall hear, that shall he **speak**: and he will **shew** you things to come"* (John 16:13).

The things that the Holy Spirit will both tell and show us are the instructions and works God preordained for us. Every human was created by God to follow the promptings of His Holy Spirit and thus fulfill their unique purpose. The Spirit of Truth is hindered because of iniquity. This is the reason many today fail to hear and see from God, and thus live a life far removed from God's original purpose.

---

[5] Again, the definition for vanity, from the *Ancient Hebrew Lexicon of the Bible* is: "The use of the power within the loins for vain or other improper purposes." Vigor is: "The power within the belly, or loins, for reproduction or creative work."

> "For we are His workmanship, created in Christ Jesus to good works, which God has before ordained that we should walk in them" (Eph. 2:10).

Much of the corruption, hypocrisy and impotence in many churches and in the lives of believers today are due to the influence of iniquity, along with the abuse and misappropriation of grace—which is more often used as a band-aid or "get-out-of-jail-free" card.

In the context of the third commandment, when we take on the Name of the Lord into our lives through faith, we are taking on the identity, character and position of all that God is. When we fail to do this, we are in effect taking the name of the Lord "in vain." The identity that God has created for each of His children will cause a person to be a legitimate child of God through obedience to His divine instructions. Anything that causes the fullness, truth and purpose of God's original intention and design to decrease in our lives is most likely contaminated by iniquity.

Manifesting His Name

When we take the name of the Lord into our lives, it comes with the vigor to manifest the fullness of His name. Jesus demonstrated this through His life on earth. He testified of it in the prayer He prayed before He completed His assignment on this earth.

> "I have glorified thee on the earth: I have finished the work which thou gavest me to do. And now, O Father, glorify thou me with thine own self with the glory which I had with thee before the world was. **I have manifested thy name** unto the men which thou gavest me out of the world: thine they were, and thou gavest them me; and they have kept thy word" (John 17:4, KJV).

My prayer is that we work to manifest the Name of God through loving righteousness and hating iniquity. Unrighteousness is defined as "being out of alignment through perversion of the will and laws of God" and disobedience is "the manifestation of the negligence or defiance of set rules."

When we fail to reveal the pure nature of God, these negative behaviors will automatically result, due to the presence of iniquity. The disciples, apostles and, of course, Jesus continually warned of such behaviors throughout the New Testament.

Additional books could be written on iniquity from an Old Testament perspective, yet throughout the entire Bible, one thing is very clear: we must love righteousness and hate iniquity if there is to be any hope in exterminating iniquity. In the following passage, we are given a clue to the remedy for iniquity.

> *"But to the Son He says, 'Your throne, O God, is forever and ever. A scepter of righteousness is the scepter of Your kingdom.* **You have loved righteousness and hated iniquity**, *therefore God, Your God, has anointed You with the oil of gladness above Your fellows'"* (Heb. 1:8-9).

[Note: In a subsequent chapter, we will explore further the keys to discovering, rooting out and ridding our lives of iniquity.]

⌘

Chapter Summary:

- Iniquity births man's wisdom, which is contrary to God's wisdom.

- As long as iniquity is in our lives, we can have *knowledge* of the Word but not the *truth* of the Word.

- Though grace is a free gift of God, its benefits come through the voice of truth, which we must obey to experience life free from iniquity.

- To be planted together in the likeness of Jesus' death requires you to daily "carry your cross". This is a requirement to following Christ. Iniquity will always cause you to loosen the grip of the cross.

- It is impossible to completely lose your life for the sake of God if iniquity is present.

- To take the name of the Lord in vain means to take God's original identity for your life and turn it into a state of vanity.

- God's voice and vision comes to us through the inner senses of our spirit: the inner eyes and inner ears.

- Every human was created by God to follow the promptings of His Holy Spirit and thus fulfill their unique purpose.

APPLICATION:

1. Prior to reading this chapter, were you aware of the teachings of the disciples and apostles on iniquity? Give some thought to how many times you were taught about the truth of iniquity in religious or non-religious environments.

2. Seek God as to whether you have accepted not only His grace but also His truth in your life, and whether you have allowed the Spirit of Truth to help you overcome iniquity.

CHAPTER 5

THE BIOLOGY AND SCIENCE OF INIQUITY

"Since God created all true biology and true science they are therefore evidence that God exists." – Julio Alvarado Jr.

With the advance of scientific research in the area of human biology, studies have begun to show that when an individual practices negative behaviors, these behaviors literally become a part of that person's biological makeup. The behaviors form patterns of thinking and actions that, if continued, eventually become part of the protein content of the individual's blood system.

For example, my family has a history of alcoholism, drug addiction and divorce. Due to our family's history, these tendencies are considered rather normal within my family and even expected. I used to be an alcoholic and drug addict and went through a divorce before becoming a Christian. Even after becoming a Christian, I found it difficult to overcome these things and nearly came to the point of a second divorce.

Iniquity of the Fathers

Dr. Pepe Ramnath, research scientist and Pastor of the Miramar Kingdom Community Centre in Miramar, Florida, states that predictable patterns of behavior are built within the complexities of human DNA. DNA (Deoxyribonucleic Acid) holds the genetic instructions for all living things, including some viruses. The main function of DNA is to hold long-term information, contained in parts of the DNA called "genes." These patterns can either be influenced by God's predestined purpose or they can be distorted through negative thinking and behaviors. The result of this is iniquity, which is transferred genetically.

In his book, *The Genetics of Vision*, Dr. Ramnath explains that inside the cells of every human being is the Golgi Apparatus. The Golgi Apparatus, also known as The Golgi Complex, are protein cells found next to the nucleus that holds the DNA. The Golgi Apparatus is responsible for directing the molecular "traffic" of information and life experiences. This information—in the form of protein in the cells—travels to the brain and throughout the brain in the vein and nerve systems, which affects the thought process of an individual. The Golgi Apparatus is designed to collect and store behaviors, histories and memories that are then transferred to the next generation through the conception process by way of the protein in the male's sperm.

During the process of conception, the blood type, structure and content of the blood—including the Golgi Apparatus—is also birthed in the child's DNA. Genes are transferable. Therefore, if we disobey the laws that God has given us, it not only affects and alters *our* thinking and actions in negative ways, but it also causes the *next generation* to become susceptible to that same disobedience.

This scientific discovery proves that a statement made thousands of years ago in the Bible, is in fact a biological process.

> "Thou shalt not bow down thyself unto them, nor serve them: for I the LORD thy God am a jealous God, visiting the iniquity of the fathers upon the children unto the third and fourth generation of them that hate me" (Ex. 20:5 and Deut. 5:9, KJV).

Dr. Ramnath makes this profound statement: "In a sense, we do not live for ourselves but for the next generation that we will eventually introduce into this world."

Dr. Ramnath states that DNA was designed to work properly by the transferring of genes to form nations, commonly called generations. This transference is accomplished through the fathers. Dr. Ramnath's observation is that, by the way *we* choose to live, we have the power to help *our children* genetically visualize a better future and destroy iniquity. We must root out iniquity from our lives and educate our children on how to do the same. Sadly, the concept of eliminating iniquity from our lives and genetic nature is foreign to most people today.

In the above Scripture, "iniquity" is defined in Hebrew as the word, âvôn. In the Ancient Hebrew Lexicon of the Bible, this word is defined as "guilt that results from twisted actions." It literally refers to one who is, as the saying goes, "Guilty by association."

Another point to notice in the above passage is that God visits the *iniquity* of the fathers, not the *sins* of the fathers. We are not responsible for the sins of our fathers, yet we are responsible to root out the iniquities of our fathers that might still be affecting us in a negative way. In other words, the reason God "visits" them is to see if someone in that generation has taken up the responsibility to root out iniquity's existence so that the family tree will no longer be affected by the ancestor's negligence.

> "The soul that sins, it shall die. The son shall not bear the iniquity of the father, nor shall the father bear the iniquity of the son. The righteousness of the righteous shall be on him, and the wickedness of the wicked shall be on him. But if the wicked will turn from all his sins which he has committed, and keep all My statutes, and do justice and right, he shall surely live; he shall not die" (Ez. 18:20-21).

The word "bear" in the above passage is defined as "to continue to lift up or grab hold of." If someone is ignorant of iniquity's presence in their life, they will unknowingly bear the effects of iniquity. In many people's lives, this is exactly what is going on. Biblically, these are called "secret iniquities" [Ps. 90:8, KJV]. Negative behavioral, mental and character issues will remain in our biological makeup unless we deal with them and root them out.

The Firstborn

One of the main reasons that Jesus came to this earth was to set us free from iniquity by giving us the cure through the cleansing of His blood and access to the provision of truth. This is why Jesus was referred to as "the first born among many" [See Rom. 8:29, Col. 1:15, Rev. 1:15].

Jesus was the only begotten (sole born) of God the Father [John 1:14]. His blood came from God Himself and as such, He was not affected by the physical transference of iniquity. God could not use the human sperm of a male, such as that of Jesus' earthly "father," Joseph. If you read Joseph's genealogy [Matt. 1:1-16], you will notice plenty of iniquity transference and conduct in Joseph's bloodline.

Jesus had—and still has—the only pure, sinless bloodline, as it came from God Himself. Therefore, by accepting and applying the power of His blood—not only by confession from the mouth but more importantly by proper application and obedience—we have the potential to cancel the effects of the iniquity of all past generations on our lives. We will read more on this in a subsequent chapter.

Another powerful insight that you must capture at this moment is that when you properly appropriate the blood of Jesus into your life, you get the Golgi Apparatus of God. In other words, you get the complex "traffic" of *truth* information—the genes, character, behaviors, histories, and the very memories—of God Himself. This is the secret of what made Jesus so "Father-conscious." I will expound on this vital process and truth in a more detailed way in my next book. This phenomenon is linked to a book that has been prewritten about your life that is authored by God Himself, a book that very few people are aware of.

Jesus was the biggest "copycat" that the world has ever known. All He did was copy what He heard and saw from His Father. This is the same process that every human being is also supposed to duplicate.

God has the entire blueprint of our being. He can show us how to break the genetic codes of iniquity that we have inherited from our forefathers. Ever since the fall of man through the first Adam in the garden, humans have been exposed to the contaminant of iniquity. Since all humans came from Adam's sperm, we are all offspring of Adam. The good news is that ever since the birth and resurrection of whom the Bible calls the last Adam (Jesus), we have a remedy for iniquity [1 Cor. 15:45].

Dr. Caroline Leaf is a neuroscientist who has studied the brain for over 30 years. In her book *Who Switched off My Brain?* Dr. Leaf further explains the effect of our negative thinking and behaviors through what she has called "toxic thoughts." In her book, Dr. Leaf talks about "neuroplasticity," which is the brain's ability to form new connections and reorganize itself structurally and functionally back to a healthy state of being. This restructuring is possible even when the brain has been affected negatively by one's upbringing or environment, or by a traumatic injury.

Dr. Leaf refutes the myth that our natural genes shape who we are. Scientific research has begun to prove that the thoughts that we have—of ourselves and others—determine which genes are activated within us. We do not have to fall back on the victimized mentality of, "It runs in my family and it's impossible to change this." Someone who has a history of negative behavior in their bloodline can make a conscious decision, backed up with actions, to change not only their life, but also their present and future family tree, by refusing to repeat their forefathers' history.

Each one of us is created in the image and likeness of God. Every person on this earth came out of Adam through natural birth. However, every born-again believer has the potential to be released from the grip of iniquity. We have access to the spiritual genetics that can overcome the iniquity introduced into this world through the wrong decisions of the first Adam. We have the power to allow our spiritual genes to shape us. Yet all too often we continue to allow our natural genes to shape us.

In her book, Dr. Leaf points out that the new scientific discovery of Epigenetics (which teaches that our perceptions and life experiences remodel our genes, not the other way around) has changed the conventional understanding of genetic control. It argues against the traditional belief that our natural genes control everything, including behavior and emotions. We don't have to be the victims of our human biology if we would just understand the power of our spiritual genealogy. Even though our natural disposition has been transferred to us from previous generations, they no longer have the power to shape us if we choose to claim our spiritual birthright.

We need to take control of our thoughts, choices, actions, behaviors and influences—including the words that we speak to ourselves and the words that are spoken to us. When we allow these things to negatively influence us, we are repeating these natural negative tendencies for ourselves and our children. Dr. Leaf's research teaches that "toxic thoughts" in our brains lead to emotional, physical and spiritual malfunctions of the human body. Iniquity is in reality the toxic waste that corrupts every aspect of our lives.

Biology or Iniquity?

One of the manifestations of iniquity that we are seeing today is homosexuality and lesbianism. The widespread pressure of just a small number of people has succeeded in altering public perception and is continuing to gain strength to where laws are being changed to accommodate its existence and practice.

This book is not meant to single out any particular lifestyle. Whether someone is guilty of sexual lust for the opposite sex, or is what the Bible calls a fornicator (one who has sex out of the context of marriage) or is an adulterer, all of these are sins and manifestations of iniquity. All are equally wrong and immoral according to God.

No human being is born or "destined" to be a homosexual or a lesbian. I want to make it clear that I am in no way suggesting that is there is such a thing as a homosexual gene that determines your sexual preference. God did not create humans with a homosexual or lesbian gene. Though the Golgi Apparatus does give some insight as to why homosexuality or lesbianism might be in the genealogy of a family, the reality is that it did not originate in God. It originated instead in the character and behavior of the current or prior generations.

Whether one has chosen to believe the lie that they are born with such a *predestined* gene or one blatantly chooses homosexuality or lesbianism as a lifestyle, the fact remains that you can become born again. Becoming born again, according to the proper understanding and application of it's original purpose, will introduce you to the reality that God never intended for homosexuality or lesbianism to be a part of your life, or the life of any human being for that matter.

Much of homosexuality and lesbianism is rooted in negligence and abuse, often from a male figure in someone's past. I have personally counseled with men and have knowledge of many women whose life stories contain experiences of someone, usually a male, sexually abusing them. Many of these individuals link that abuse in their past as the reason they have chosen the "gay lifestyle." Many others probably haven't made that connection.

Many people today, even within the church, are either practicing or struggling with the thoughts of homosexuality. The Bible is very clear that homosexuality, which includes lesbianism, is an abomination to God. Bisexuality is also practicing homosexuality, since it is the desire to have sexual relations with someone of the same gender.

"You shall not lie with mankind as with womankind. It is abomination to God" (Lev. 18:22).

> *"If a man also lies with mankind, as he lies with a woman, both of them have committed an abomination. They shall surely be put to death. Their blood shall be on them"* (Lev. 20:13).

The word "abomination" in these verses literally means "disgusting." The unlawful and ungodly practice of homosexuality is mentioned in the moral laws of the Old Testament, which still apply today. The penalty for breaking this moral law in Old Testament times was outlined in Leviticus 18:29: "For whosoever shall commit any of these abominations, even the souls that commit them shall be cut off from among their people." This was God's law, yet today we are encouraged to embrace what is now called an "alternative" lifestyle.

In the New Testament it is also mentioned, yet with more severe consequences. We can see the consequences of homosexuality in the following passages.

> *"Do you not know that the unrighteous shall not inherit the kingdom of God? Do not be deceived; neither fornicators, nor idolaters, nor adulterers, nor abusers, nor homosexuals, nor thieves, nor covetous, nor drunkards, nor revilers, nor extortioners, shall inherit the kingdom of God. And such were some of you. But you are washed, but you are sanctified, but you are justified in the name of the Lord Jesus, and by the Spirit of our God"* (1 Cor. 6:9-11).

The above passage doesn't single out homosexuality. My point here in focusing on homosexuality is due to the strong mindset that comes with it. Many practicing homosexuals today believe that God made them that way and that God understands their desires and behaviors. They state that, since God is a God of love, "Me and my partner love each other, so this is acceptable in the eyes of God."

Practicing any type of sin and justifying its presence in your life by believing the lie that God is ok with it will result in a severe consequence. The consequence is that God will allow you to give in to your desires, which leads to what the Bible calls a "reprobate mind." Reprobate means "what is unapproved, rejected, worthless, and castaway."

The following passages in the book of Romans help us understand the grave consequences of any attempt to change the truth of God's law in order to believe that sinful behavior or lifestyle is acceptable.

> "Because, knowing God, they did not glorify Him as God, neither were thankful. But they became vain in their imaginations, and their foolish heart was darkened. Professing to be wise, they became fools and changed the glory of the incorruptible God into an image made like corruptible man, and birds, and four-footed animals, and creeping things. **Therefore God also gave them up to uncleanness through the lusts of their hearts, to dishonor their own bodies between themselves**" (Rom. 1:21-24).

> "For they changed the truth of God into a lie, and they worshiped and served the created thing more than the Creator, who is blessed forever. Amen. For this cause, God gave them up to dishonorable affections. **For even their women changed the natural use into that which is against nature. And likewise also the men, leaving the natural use of the woman, burned in their lust toward one another; males with males working out shamefulness, and receiving in themselves the recompense which was fitting for their error**" (Rom. 1:25-27).

> "And even as they did not think fit to have God in their knowledge, **God gave them over to a reprobate mind, to do the things not right**, being filled with all unrighteousness, fornication, wickedness, covetousness, maliciousness; being full of envy, murder, quarrels, deceit, evil habits, becoming whisperers, backbiters, haters of God,

insolent, proud, braggarts, inventors of evil things, disobedient to parents, undiscerning, perfidious, without natural affection, unforgiving, unmerciful; who, knowing the righteous order of God, **that those practicing such things are worthy of death, not only do them, but have pleasure in those practicing them**" (Rom. 1:28-32).

Mercy and forgiveness are available from God through Jesus Christ once people position themselves to truly repent and change their mind, behavior and lifestyle to accept the truth of who God created them to be.

Homosexuality is arguably one of the strongest mental strongholds that a person can experience. This is evidenced in men trying to behave like women in their body language, voice and even how they dress, and women desiring to act like men. It can literally affect the physiology, chemistry and actions of the entire body. The attempts to tamper with gender, physically—through the injections of hormones or surgery—or mentally—through thinking and acting like the opposite gender—is literally attempting to exchange "truth" for a lie.

In the context of iniquity versus the truth of living who you were ordained to be, homosexuality cannot be given any other description than "iniquitized." If you were born a male, you must function as a male, otherwise you will never reproduce or create the work that for which you were predestined and originally designed. If a man chooses to function as a woman, he would be using his body and mind in vain, and for improper uses. The same applies to a female attempting to function as a male.

In my blood family, numerous relatives presently practice the gay lifestyle, or practiced it at some point in their past. Due to my strong cocaine addiction, in my late teens I made a decision to prostitute my body to a homosexual drug dealer. For about one year I traded cocaine for sex approximately a dozen times to a man. This was one of the darkest times in my life, and a decision that I still regret today. Though my desire has never been to lead a homosexual lifestyle, the reality is that I practiced homosexual activity; therefore, I was still guilty of the sin.

This was one secret of my life that for many years I was ashamed to share. It remains one of the most embarrassing things that I have ever done. Even though I didn't know God at this time in my life, I still remember the perception that what I was doing was morally wrong. Deep in my soul, I still had a level of conscience—the voice of God that exists in every human being—telling me the difference between right and wrong.

Since making the decision to discover and root out any form of iniquity in my life, whether it was transferred to me generationally or I caused it myself, I have decided to be completely transparent about my past and present. To my surprise, rather than being ostracized or labeled, as I opened the door of my heart to share these personal experiences, many have openly confessed to me similar experiences in their own lives. Their opening up to confess these buried secrets in their lives has started a healing and restoration process for them as well. *God's truth holds great power to overcome secrets, lies, sins and iniquity.*

Our bodies are supposed to be what I call "Containers of Truth." When we actively choose to reproduce and create all that God has in store for us, we will become a solution to the problems in the world, rather than creating an additional problem. We will become a force for good, rather than a proponent for iniquity.[6]

⌘

---

[6] The word "science" is defined simply as "knowledge." Biology is defined as "the study of life." The work of scientists Dr. Leaf and Dr. Ramnath, which combines modern research with spiritual insights, brings a clearer understanding of the inner workings of human biological mindsets to validate the effects of iniquity on the human race. I am grateful to them for their work and insight. Their contact information can be found in the appendix.

CHAPTER SUMMARY:

- Spiritual iniquity is taking the power of the truth that God places within the loins of the mind and using it for vain or unintended purposes rather than using it for its intended creative or reproductive work.

- Physical iniquity is the physical manifestation of ungodly character and behavior unintended by God, which becomes part of the physiology of a person.

- Disobedience to God's laws affects and alters not only our thinking and actions in negative ways, but it also causes the next generation to be susceptible to that same disobedience.

- The blood of Jesus introduces the spiritual Golgi Apparatus of God into your life, which contains the complex "traffic" of *truth*: information, genes, character, behaviors, histories, and even the memories of God Himself.

- Physical iniquity has the potential to introduce toxic thoughts and behaviors into our lives.

- We don't have to be the victims of our human biology if we understand the power of our spiritual genealogy.

- Homosexuality is one of the strongest mental strongholds that a person can experience. In the context of iniquity versus the truth of striving to become who you were ordained to be, homosexuality cannot be given any other description than "iniquitized."

The Biology and Science of Iniquity

APPLICATION:

1. Take time to consider your newfound knowledge of the Golgi Apparatus as it pertains to the DNA structure of your biological makeup that came from your biological father.

2. Since the original purpose of the Golgi Apparatus is to introduce the complex "traffic" of truth information—the genes, character, behaviors, histories, and the very memories of the individual whose seed you came from—consider the possibilities of what your life can become by allowing the Golgi Apparatus of God, your spiritual Father, to influence your future.

3. Spend some time thinking about your personal family history, taking note of any negative tendencies or practices that "run" in your family. Now that you have acquired this knowledge and perhaps newfound perspective about iniquity, ask yourself whether you truly believe that you can be completely set free from these issues through the cleansing power of Christ.

4. If you know of someone who is struggling with the thoughts or practice of homosexuality or lesbianism, encourage them to read this book so that they can grasp the root knowledge and understanding of why they are having such thoughts and/or practicing such a lifestyle.

Chapter 6

INIQUITY OF THE FATHERS TRANSFERRED

"A nation or civilization that continues to produce soft-minded men purchases its own spiritual death on an installment plan." – Martin Luther King, Jr.

In review, spiritual iniquity is taking the power of the truth that God places within the loins of the mind and using it for vain or unintended purposes rather than using it for its intended creative or reproductive work.

Physical iniquity is the physical manifestation of ungodly character and behavior, which becomes part of the physiology of a person.

Spiritual iniquity will always produce physical iniquity and physical iniquity will always be rooted in spiritual iniquity.

Physical iniquity originates, and is transferred, through the male. In the definition of the word "vigor" found in the *Ancient Hebrew Lexicon of the Bible*, we find that the words "belly" and "loins" are mentioned. In the physical sense, the belly of a female is known as the source or starting place of the fetus or unborn child. In the male, the "loins" can also be a reference to a male's sperm sack or container.

When a woman becomes pregnant, a fetus is produced in her belly. This fetus will eventually grow into a child. Though a child is made by a male and female, it is a creation of God.

Raise up a Child

Failing to understand the purpose for something will invariably result in that thing's misuse and/or abuse. This concept can be applied to childrearing. We have already explored that the word sin is defined as "to miss the mark." In failing to understand the unique, God-ordained purpose for a child, parents will most likely "miss the mark" by failing to raise the child along the lines of his or her purpose.

Jesse, the father of King David, did not have a clue that his youngest son was destined to be a king; therefore he didn't raise him to be one. This fact is recorded in the story of the prophet Samuel being sent by God to the house of Jesse to anoint David, the successor of King Saul. Jesse presented seven of his sons to the prophet and failed to mention that he had an eighth son [See 1 Sam. 16:1-13]. If Jesse would have had insight into the purpose of his son, he would not have even presented the older seven sons. His response to Samuel would have been, "I know exactly which of my sons you came to anoint as king."

Some historians and theologians believe that King David was born out of wedlock and that this was the reason his father failed to present David to the prophet. I don't believe that this was the case. I believe that his parents birthed him into this world without any knowledge about his God-given identity and purpose. Evidently David was predestined to be a king otherwise God would never have chosen him. His parents "conceived him in sin" in missing the mark of who God created King David to be; his life was therefore shaped in iniquity due to the absence or misapplied truth about his life.

*"Behold, I was **shapen in iniquity**; and **in sin did my mother conceive me"** (Ps. 51:5, KJV).*

A revelation I received not long ago came from an opportunity that I was given to speak on a topic called "Father Wounds." As I was studying and researching for my talk, two portions of scriptures related to parenting caught my attention.

The first one is found in Matthew 1:18-22 and Luke 1:26-35. The second one is found in Luke 1:5-17. In these passages, an angel named Gabriel sent by God gave Mary and Joseph—the earthly parents of Jesus—and Zacharias—the father of John the Baptist—*vital information*. In both cases they were told the identity and purpose of their child, as well as what name their child was to be given. In other words, they were given what I call "inside information" about their respective children. In other words, they received "truth" about who they were bringing forth into the world. Evidently King David's parents did not have the "inside information" of who King David was born to become.

Due to this vital information that their parents received straight from Heaven, Jesus and John would have been raised by their parents with principles, instruction and direction to prepare them for their God-given purpose, so that they would be prepared to fulfill it when the time came.

A verse that is commonly used to raise children in the church today is, "Train up a child in the way he should go; and when he is old, he will not depart from it" (Pro. 22:6, KJV).

The "it" in this passage refers to the child's unique purpose. This is the same word used before Jesus' last breath on the cross when he said, "It is finished" (John 19:30). The "it" that Jesus was referring to was His purpose and mission on the earth.

The phrase "the way" is a reference to one's mission on earth. The word "way" is defined as "a course of life or mode of action." A Hebraic translation of this word is "a prescribed path." Both Jesus' and John's parents had insight into the pre-scribed or prewritten path for each of them.

How different this world would be today if every parent would take the time to hear from God and ask the Creator what to name their child, and what their child's purpose is. If parents did all they could to equip their child to fulfill his or her specific purpose, the world would be full of purpose driven and focused individuals making a positive difference in the world.

So many people today—young people and adults—suffer from a perpetual identity crisis because they were raised without this vital information; they have lived most, if not all, of their lives without even being aware that their life has a unique purpose and plan.

Biblically, iniquity was conceived and birthed into the world through Lucifer. The first transfer of spiritual iniquity happened to Adam and Eve in the Garden of Eden when Satan, in the form of a serpent, distorted the truth of God's command to not eat of the tree of the knowledge of good and evil [See Gen. 2:16-17, 3:1-6].

Adam and Eve were without iniquity until the exchange between themselves and the serpent. They were perfect in all their ways, just like Lucifer was, from the day that they were created until iniquity was found in them [Ez. 28:15]. Since God is a God of truth and no iniquity at all is found in Him, when He created them by His Spirit and made Adam from the dust of the ground and Eve from the rib of Adam, the same was true of them. They had authority. They were fully equipped, mature, whole, and lacking nothing. They were made in the image and likeness of God. One disobedient act, one transaction with the devil, caused their departure from their God-given purpose and an end to the intimate relationship that Adam and Eve had with God.

Though Eve ate the forbidden fruit first, it wasn't until Adam—the male—ate the fruit that sin was introduced into this world. Today it is still through the male that iniquity is being birthed into this world and transferred from generation to generation. Transference occurs due to a lack of truth from the Holy Spirit, or due to disobedience if this truth is known. These conditions result in displacement from the perfect (mature) position that all humans are predestined to have in God.

Throughout the Bible, and even today, the male is meant to be the foundation of the family. The male is supposed to create an environment where the family structure can learn about God. He is meant to help lead the members of his family to find the specific will God for their lives.

A Primary Responsibility

It was the responsibility of the male then, as well as now, to introduce, sustain and strengthen the knowledge of God in the family structure. A man can provide for his family with food, clothing, shelter, finances and other needs, but if he fails to provide for his family spiritually, he has failed in his most important task.

If a father fails to accomplish this vital responsibility, then what he transfers to his children is ignorance of the most important aspect of life: the knowledge of God. This is the root cause of the family deterioration that is happening in the world today, especially in the western hemisphere.

Families today are being forced to operate without the proper foundation of a Godly father, which is God's planned structure for the family. Men who fail to undertake this God-ordained responsibility are manifesting a form of hating God. The First Commandment given to humanity contains insight to this reality.

> "Thou shalt have no other gods before me. Thou shalt not make unto thee any graven image, or any likeness of anything that is in heaven above, or that is in the earth beneath, or that is in the water under the earth: Thou shalt not bow down thyself to them, nor serve them: for I the LORD thy God am a jealous God, visiting the iniquity of the fathers upon the children unto the third and fourth generation of them that hate me; and shewing mercy unto

thousands of them that love me, and keep my commandments" (Ex. 20:3-6, KJV).

"Thou shalt have no other gods before me" is not just a reference to idol worship as traditionally taught. Humans are also considered "gods" [See Ps. 82:6]. When a man fails to put God first in his life, he becomes a god unto himself, in essence putting himself before God the Almighty. He is also guilty of being a source of iniquity that is then transferred to the generations that follow him.

One only has to journey through the Bible to discover the vital importance of the man's influence on the family structure. The male was instrumental and mandated by God to be the protector, provider and visionary of the family. One of his primary roles was to make sure that the Word of the Lord was not just introduced to the family but that the principles of God's Word were applied to their daily living. Key men like Moses, Noah, and Joseph—amongst many other examples—were responsible to hear from God in order to create or reproduce some plan of deliverance or salvation for their families and loved ones.

Today this vital responsibility has been lost or, at best, passed off to the local church, a pastor, television minister, or some other type of spiritual leader. Many men have lost the art of hearing the voice of God and have allowed others to be the voice of God to them and their families. If I, as a father, don't know God for myself or if I claim to know God but don't hear God's clear voice, how can I accurately teach my children what I myself don't know? Men are responsible to intimately know God, to hear His voice, and to teach their sons and daughters to do the same.

I don't want to ignore the value of the female in the family structure, especially in western cultures such as the United States where many women have been forced to take the roles of leader, provider, protector and visionary of the family due to the man's absence. Even when the male is physically present, many families have had to default to the female as the spiritual head of the home, in cases where the father is failing to take up his God-ordained responsibilities. A look into many churches today will prove that more women are in attendance than men.

Though I'm thankful for the women taking on these vital roles and responsibilities, the reality is that the family structure has been weakened due to fathers being physically or spiritually absent from the family structure.

The prisons in the United States are filled with men that were either raised by a single mother or were raised by a father that did not function in his God-designed role. In the United States, statistics show that there are about two million people in some form of prison system. Roughly 85% of those in prison were raised in fatherless homes, and these numbers are growing at an alarming rate.

Statistics also show that 90% of runaways, 63% of youth who commit suicide, 85% of youth who are in juvenile detentions systems, 71% of high school dropouts, 75% of all adolescent patients in chemical abuse centers and 80% of rapists motivated with displaced anger, all come from fatherless homes. I don't believe that these high numbers are just a coincidence; these are the effect that a father's absence has in the building, or breaking, of future generations.

A "Real Man"

Today men are responsible for more abortions than women. They are aborting the ideas and purposes of God for their lives, creating a cycle where men fail to recognize and fulfill their unique purpose, and pass this tendency on to the next generation.

A large percentage of today's youth are growing up without the vital placement of a father in their lives, leaving them to be raised by single mothers. These women do their best to provide for, protect and raise their children in loving homes; in some cases they have been very successful. However, the best way to teach a young male how to become a real man is for a real man to do the teaching. A real man is one who is functioning in the accuracy and reality of the image and likeness of God [See Gen. 1:26].

My definition of a "real man" has changed over the years. When I was younger, to me a real man was one who turned a legal age (such as the age of 21 in the United States). Later, a real man for me was one who took responsibility by taking care of himself without the help of his parents. These were false understandings of what a real man was.

One of the major sources of enlightenment on this topic that God sent my way was a book written by Dr. Myles Munroe entitled *Understanding the Purpose and Power of Men*. I have personally given away over 100 copies of this book to men that I have encountered since my "conversion." I recommend that every man read this book. Dr. Munroe has also written a female version of this book called *Understanding the Purpose and Power of Women*, which I have also read. These two resources are "must reads" to gain a better understanding of why God created the male and female as well as how to appreciate, understand, value and treat one another.

After reading these books, I quickly realized how deficient I was in my knowledge of what a real man was. This set me on a journey to acquire more knowledge, understanding, and wisdom, which has radically improved my potential as a man of God, as father to my children and as husband to my wife.

My current definition of a real man will not be found in *Webster's Dictionary* or in any encyclopedia. I have developed this definition from key principles found in the Bible. A real man is "one who has an intimate relationship with his original source of life: God. He has no identity issues from his past or present that keep him from functioning productively in life. His purpose has been revealed to him by God Himself. He has a clear vision for his life and God has given him a detailed plan, which he has turned into his mission in life."

In my opinion, anything less than this is simply a male. A real man is one who has decided to no longer function as a "son of man," which is one who allows male influence, the media, society or any other earthly resource to dictate and shape his life. A real man is actively pursuing to be a "son of God" through hearing the voice of God and demonstrating complete obedience in all things to God, our Father in Heaven.

Living one's true reality is derived from what God has preordained that life to be; that information can only be received from Him. God is the one who created each person; therefore no other source on earth is authorized to outline this vital information.

No human is authorized to tell you who you are since they did not create you; God did. Your parents can't even claim this right; they might have *made* you, but God *created* you. Your parents may exercise naming rights and give you your name, but God holds the claim and right in identifying you.

If every parent on earth were to ask God what to name their child based on their predestined purpose, I imagine many of us would have been given a different name. For instance, I was named after my father, so I'm "Julio Jr." Julio means July in Spanish, yet the month of July does not identify me. What God has told me about my life and purpose is what identifies me.

The issue is not necessarily what you are named. The issue and major problem is that many people don't understand who they really are in Christ. They have not come to the knowledge of their predestined, God-ordained identity. This information is foundational in understanding your true purpose on earth.

This process of getting clear, predestined identity was modeled in the prophet Jeremiah's life.

> "The word of the LORD came to me, saying, 'Before I formed you in the womb I knew you, before you were born I set you apart; I appointed you as a prophet to the nations'" (Jer. 1:4-5, NIV).

God inspired King David to write about humanity's process in the following verses, which are keys to understanding life as it is meant to be:

> "For you created my inmost being; you knit me together in my mother's womb. I praise you because I am fearfully and wonderfully made; your works are wonderful, I know that full well. My frame was not hidden from you when I was made in the secret place, when I was woven together in the depths of the earth. Your eyes saw my unformed body; all the days ordained for me were written in your book before one of them came to be. How precious to me are your thoughts, God! How vast is the sum of them" (Ps. 139:13-17).

Even the best parents in this world, with all their love and good intentions, can miss the mark. They can "sin" if they fail to lead their children to connect with the Creator, God Himself.

This was a primary role of the male in the Bible and still should be a primary role of the male today [Prov. 22:6]. The male is responsible to make sure that his family and children eventually come to know God for themselves so that they can consistently build their own lifelong relationship with God [Lev. 10:11, Deut. 4:10, 6:7, 11:19].

Biblically, many men failed. King Saul, a man handpicked by God to lead his people, fell to his own selfish ways that led to his own suicide and the death of those around him, including his son Jonathan. King David not only committed adultery but also impregnated Bathsheba and masterminded the plot to have her husband killed to cover his sinful behavior. Jacob was deceitful in his daily living. Saul, whom we now know as Paul, was a self-righteous religious leader who used his power to cause the murder of innocent believers.

Chapters could be written about many other men from the Bible that failed, some of whom died as failures. Yet some of these men encountered God in an aggressive way, causing them to turn their lives around and become the successes of whom we still talk about today. The ones that became success stories are the ones who allowed God to lead them through an internal identity change, which began a process of removing the iniquity from their lives.

When a man is unaware of who he truly is according to his predestined state in Christ, his behaviors will reflect his ignorance through many forms such as pride, rebellion, disobedience towards authority, drug and alcohol addiction, abuse towards women and children, laziness, passiveness and complacency—just to name a few. These types of behaviors are present even in many of the men in churches and world governments today. Each one of us is created by God to be successful in every area of our life. Yet many men fail to experience this success due to an overwhelming lack of "real men" teaching, modeling and representing accurate manhood through their daily living.

The Need for Spiritual Fathers

Though I'm sure that there are environments where men are successfully being taught how to live righteously, past and current statistics tell the story that there are not enough healthy environments where a man can learn how to live in the fullness of who he is predesigned by God to be. Many men today are also suffering from "father wounds," which results from the influence of a father figure that was either absent or inaccurate in his fathering skills due to the presence of iniquity in his life.

One of the functions of the prophets Elijah and John the Baptist was to return the hearts of the children back to their fathers [Mal. 4:5-6, Luke 1:13-17]. In my opinion, any modern-day prophet bears this same responsibility. If the hearts of the fathers are still contaminated with iniquitized thinking, behaviors and lifestyle, what healthy role models do the children have to follow?

What our children and underdeveloped men need today are spiritual fathers. We have plenty of instructors in the world today. Many men are guilty of trying to *instruct* their children, yet failing to accurately *father* them due to the iniquity in their lives. The Apostle

Paul was well aware of the shortage of fathers when he was inspired by God to pen the following words to the people in Corinth:

> *"I do not write these things to shame you, but as my beloved children I warn you. For though you have ten thousand instructors in Christ, yet you do not have many fathers; for I have begotten you in Christ Jesus through the gospel. Therefore I beseech you, be imitators of me"* (1 Cor. 4:14-16).

Paul is a great example of not just a great teacher but, more importantly, a great spiritual father. Tradition teaches that Paul had no biological children, yet we know he had spiritual sons such as Timothy and Titus. Paul is a great example to prove that you do not have to have biological children to father children and men. Paul was a source, sustainer and a foundation of the Gospel of the Kingdom of God, which he shared with the men that he had begotten in Christ. Just like a great father, he encouraged his spiritual sons to imitate him.

Paul had a radical encounter with God which changed his identity and function in life back to God's original plan for him. Paul removed all forms of iniquity in his life, qualifying him to encourage all he was exposed to, "Be imitators of me, even as I also am of Christ" (1 Cor. 11:1). This world doesn't need more sperm donors who just produce children; this world needs men who are willing to be obedient sons to God the Father, which qualifies them to be accurate fathers on this earth. Accurate fathers teach by their words and actions and are an example and conduit of God; what they hear and see from God, they transfer to those whom God has entrusted to them.

⌘

CHAPTER SUMMARY:

- Spiritual iniquity will always produce physical iniquity and physical iniquity will always be rooted in spiritual iniquity.

- Failing to understand the purpose for something will invariably result in that thing's misuse and/or abuse. This includes childrearing.

- In order to accurately "Train up a child in the way he/she should go" so that "when he/she is old, he/she will not depart from it," one must receive the inside information from God Himself as to the "Way" (the course of life that is pre-scribed/prewritten) and the "It" (the purpose/assignment) of the child.

- A real man is one has decided to no longer function as a "son of man" but is actively pursuing to function as a "son of God" by learning to hear the voice of God and demonstrating complete obedience in all things to God.

- Many men today are suffering from "father wounds," which results from the influence of a father figure that was either absent or inaccurate in his fathering skills due to iniquity.

- A primary responsibility of every father figure is to be an example of a "son of God" and to raise his children in the nurture, admonition and true knowledge of God.

Application:

1. If you are a man: take time to pray and ask God if you are striving to be a "son of God" and what steps you can take to grow in that area.

2. If you are a father: reflect on whether you are striving to fulfill your vital responsibility of imparting to your children the knowledge of God.

3. If you are a parent: take time to seek God as to His plan for your children and construct a spirit-led plan as to how to help your child/children prepare for their original God-ordained purpose.

Chapter 7

The Iniquities of You and Me

"When you discover iniquity in you, what you have discovered is my identity, purpose, vision, mission and voice in you." – Satan

Once I made the discovery of the root meaning of iniquity, I began to work on rooting it out of my personal life. Some of my iniquities have had a stronger hold on my life than others and have required more work to root out and overcome. I have classified these particular iniquities as "strongholds." They are the ones that, if I'm not vigilant, have the potential to replant themselves in my life very easily. Though these may be called sins, the root cause of any ungodly character or behavior (whether you prefer to call it sin, lawlessness, transgression, rebellion, or any other negative word) is iniquity.

I believe that Satan has no problem with you dealing with your sin—the *fruit* or manifestation of iniquity. What he doesn't want you to deal with is the *root* of sin, which is iniquity. As long as the root is present, the fruit of it will eventually re-grow and manifest itself.

In a previous chapter, "The Biology and Science of Iniquity," we discovered that within the male sperm is the Golgi Apparatus, which collects and stores generations of behaviors, histories and memories that will be transferred to the next generation through the protein contained in it.

I believe that God originally designed this protein within the Golgi Apparatus to transfer positive traits, behaviors and information. But when a person doesn't live by the voice of truth—by ignorance or choice—the result will always be ungodly, iniquitized behavior that will surely rule the person's life and affect and infect those that they have influence over.

Generations of Iniquity

My family recently got together for a rare family reunion during a Mother's Day celebration. This type of reunion in my family has only taken place twice in the past 19 years, with the first one taking place at my wedding to my wife Ivette. We took a family photo on both occasions. The second and most recent photo included new family members who had not yet been born when the first family photo was taken. In the second photo there were 26 people, including my two older sisters and one younger brother. What amazed me about the second photo was that, because I could visually see the new additions to my family tree and I had knowledge about each individual's life, I was able to piece together a shocking fact.

Biblically, a generation can be defined as about 40 years. Although there were 26 people in the photo, there were 33 "generations" of time present since seven of us, including myself, were over the age of 40. In other words, each individual present either already began bearing children, or had the potential to do so; as such, each person was the source of their own biological generation—the people who would come after them. Out of the 26 people in my family photo, five generations have been affected by physical abuse, 14 generations have been affected by alcoholism, 15 generations have been affected by drug addiction, 10 generations have been affected by homosexuality or lesbianism, 18 generations have been affected by the addiction of smoking, 8 generations (of the 10 youth present under the age of 18 years old) were without a father figure in their lives, 11 generations are currently engaged in fornication, 17 generations have been affected by divorce, 16 out of the 26 people were born to unmarried parents. Ultimately, all 26 people have been affected by a lack of truth knowledge and identity—that which God originally preordained for them to have and live by. All of this started from one man, my biological father. All of these problems were evident either in my dad's biology or apparent in the three generations before him.

In my own past, I have been affected by drug and alcohol addiction, for which I spent four sessions of inpatient treatment. I have also been affected by cigarette addiction, pornography, habitual lying, greed, homosexual prostitution, fornication, adultery, divorce, improper childrearing, and, of course, a lack of truth knowledge and true identity. Some of these, I believe, were transferred to me biologically through my dad; some of them I was guilty of conceiving and birthing myself. In addition to the above, there are many more manifestations of iniquity that I and my family have been guilty of; I just wanted to mention some of the main ones as a case in point.

My father passed away five months before I completed the rough draft of this book. He was in my life for almost one year prior to his death. Before that, he had been absent from playing an active role in my life for over 34 years. During his last year, I had a few opportunities to communicate openly with him. For the first time, he opened his heart and I grew to understand why he made some of the life choices that he did. One of the things that he shared with me was that he and his own father never had a healthy relationship; his father never once told him that he loved him. My father basically duplicated how he was raised when he fathered me and my siblings. Although I knew that my father loved me, he never orally told me that he loved me.

I don't blame my father at all for any of the problems in my life that I mentioned above. Of course, I wished that it would have been different but I've forgiven him as well as my forefathers. I have no resentment towards them and have come to the resolution that I'm not going to let anything in my genealogical or biological history determine what the rest of my life is going to look like. It doesn't matter who fathered me naturally or what family I was born into; what matters are the choices I make to become a "new creation" in Christ Jesus and to allow the cleansing blood of Jesus and the nurturing power of the Word of God to recreate me into who I am meant to be. In other words, with God's power I am well on my way to becoming who I was supposed to be all along.

The discovery and removal of the effects of iniquity in my life have given me the opportunity to change my family tree. You have the same opportunity. You can decide today to not be a victim of the biology of your family bloodline. In fact, you have the power to change the very structure of your thinking and behaviors. You can also lead those you have influence over to do the same.

The flip side is also true, and practiced all too often in the world today. Through rejecting the knowledge of God for your life—either ignorantly or knowingly—you become an initiator of iniquity. With this knowledge, I now see how I have also transferred the iniquity that was transferred to me from my dad as well as the iniquity I originated, to my son Valentino as well to my daughters, Amaris and Ashley. I have asked them for forgiveness and apologized for not being the father that I could have been to them had I known better. They have forgiven me. Though I never intended to hurt them in any way, I must also accept the responsibility that they deserved a father who more accurately and fully lived the written and spoken commandments of God than I had for many years of my life.

I am currently in what I call a "search and rescue" mode. Though my children are adults now, I'm still responsible to search out those areas that I was deficient in due to iniquity and to improve and rescue my relationships with them so that I can more accurately father them while I am still on this earth.

I have applied this same process to my relationship with my wife. I have asked her to forgive me and have apologized for my failure to be the best husband that I could be to her. My search and rescue mission with her has the goal of being the most accurate man that she has ever seen. This goal is based on the principle and mandate that all husbands are required by God to fulfill: to love our wives as Christ loves the church [See Eph. 5:25-29]. Anything less is unacceptable. The only way to accurately and purely accomplish this is to remain free of iniquity.

How can I love my wife as Christ loves the church if I'm not washing her with the water of the Word of God? "Word" in this mandate to all husbands is the Hebrew word *ruach*, which means the verbally spoken word of God. In other words, I have to hear the voice of God for my marriage to make sure that it is without spot, blemish or wrinkle—symptoms that signify that something that is wrong. If iniquity is present in my life, it will hinder the voice of God, causing contaminants to be present in my marriage. Iniquity is the root cause of all marriage failures.

Complete unity cannot be accomplished in a marriage as long as iniquity is allowed to remain. Let me also stress that I must first wash *myself* with the water of the Word of God before I attempt to do the same for my wife.

The Power of Truth

> "Since my discovery of the fact that the language of God is Truth, I made a life-changing decision to acquire the services of His only authorized speech therapist. His name is the The Spirit of Truth."
> – Julio Alvarado Jr.

Truth from the mouth of God is needed to root out iniquity, and God provides detailed instructions to root out all marital issues, including the character flaws and behaviors that we bring into the marriage before saying "I do." One of the principles that I teach in the men's ministry in which I am involved is that all men are environment changers. As a man, you are responsible to bring accurate change into your marriage and family, even in the areas of deficiency and damage that were caused before you met your spouse (and children, should there be children already present at the time of getting married). You cannot accurately accomplish this without the unhindered truth of God's voice instructing and guiding you to repair and restore what is damaged in your family structure.

Before discovering the root meaning of iniquity, the word "truth" was just a religious word that I used. I did not understand its significance to this present life or our eternal existence. Truth is the voice of God, the language of God, straight from the Kingdom of Heaven. Truth is the foundation of the Kingdom of God, the components of which are righteousness, peace and joy. These remain dormant unless truth develops and activates them [Rom. 14:17].

The hundreds of sins recorded in the Bible are all rooted in iniquity.[7] Just one sin that is being practiced in someone's life is one sin too many. We live in a society where sinful behaviors are accepted as normal behavior and its existence is justified one way or another. Governments around the world have created, or are in the process of creating, laws designed to accommodate sins. This mindset has even infiltrated much of the church today, resulting in a perverted view of God and His laws.

Going by the Book

Revelations 20:11-13 teaches us that we will be judged according to our works, by things that are written in a set of books. Traditionally, this scripture is taught to mean the 66 books of the Bible. However, at the time of that revelation, the "Bible" wasn't

---

[7] This link gives about 667 of different types of sin: www.amazingbible.org/Documents/Bible_Studies/Sin_list_part_6.htm

even put together with its 66 books that it contains today. Could that reference instead mean the "books" of our personal lives, books that have all of our days recorded before a single one of those days even took place?

I firmly believe that we will be judged based on the principles and the spirit of the laws that are found in the written Word of God; I also believe that the books mentioned in this passage more accurately refer to the *individual* "books" that contain the details of the works that we are predestined to accomplish. However, many fail to follow the writings of these books, as they don't even know they exist [See Ps. 139:16, Jer. 30:20, Eph. 2:10].

Due to iniquity, a majority of people on earth today—even believers—don't have knowledge of what God has written in the book of their life. God has written a "book" for each and every life—He has planned the crucial details of your identity, the inspiring truth of your purpose and the daily instructions for you in living out this purpose. The book of your life which I call "Your personal Kingdom book" is a success story and has the potential to be a "bestseller." The problem is that most people either don't know about this book at all, or they don't seek to discover what is written in that book. They instead strive to create their own book, based off of their limited knowledge and "iniquitized" hearts. In many cases, the book they create might better resemble a comic book, a fiction book, or even a horror story—a book that is not based on the true story intended by God. These stories are mere experiments in comparison to a life of purpose, and they all have sad endings.

I firmly believe that there was even a "book" in Heaven written about Jesus' life [See Heb. 10:5-7], which He acted out while on earth. He lived out His original, true, ordained story and that is why it is still a "bestseller." God was depositing the information of Jesus' personal book into Him as a boy and as a man when He consistently spent time communing with His Father in prayer. Every day, God informed Him of what was written in His book, which led to the miraculous works He did while on earth [Matt. 14:23, Mark 1:35 & 6:46, Luke 5:16, 6:12 & 9:28, John 17].

The process that Jesus experienced might have been similar to a father reading a story to his child at bedtime. Instead of fables and fantasies, God the Father was reading a true story: the exact outline and plan for Jesus' daily life. As Jesus was faithful in always "rising a great while before day" (Mark 1:35), He received His daily instructions through that time of morning prayer.[8]

Jesus informs us of the purpose and mission of the greatest thief that the world will ever know. This thief is so clever that he has in the past, and continues even now, to deceive and steal, not only from nonbelievers but, more amazingly, from believers. The thief is Satan, who uses the deceptive and illusive power of iniquity to deceive the masses so that they don't discover their "true identity" in Christ. His purpose is to ensure that the contents of the book that has already been written about you from before the foundations of the earth remain hidden.

Jesus also informs us of His purpose and mission, which one can benefit from and experience through removing iniquity from his or her life. Satan is not after your possessions. What he desires to do is to kill, steal and destroy your original identity. He wants to keep you from knowing what is written in the book of your life, which contains the information and instructions to live not only "life" but an *abundant* life.

> "The thief does not come except to steal and to kill and to destroy. I have come so that they might have life, and that they might have it more abundantly" (John 10:10).

The word "abundantly" that Jesus used in this verse is rooted in the Hebrew word *yether*. This word has a root meaning of "a righteous one who is straight and firmly holds up truth." This is

---

[8] In my next book, which I have already begun to write, I expound on this concept of *the personal book of your life* as it relates to prayer. The book is meant to teach one how to hear the voice of God and to serve as a guide to seek God's personal direction for your life. It also contains information on how Jesus prayed and "did life" as a result of His prayer life—which I have researched based off of Hebraic root words that are found in the Bible that exceed the traditional understanding of prayer.

a strange definition for a word that in our understanding simply means "to have more of." Yet this definition does make sense in that truth is the key to righteous and upright living. It is the key that gives God's children access to all that they need to fulfill their purpose on this earth. The term "more abundantly" has nothing to do with acquiring more stuff; it is more accurately a term that gives us access to the fulfillment of Ephesians 1:3: "Blessed be the God and Father of our Lord Jesus Christ, who hath blessed us with all spiritual blessings in heavenly places in Christ."

The Five Start Days

A revelation that came to me while writing this book was the importance of understanding what I call the five start days. This revelation helped me to understand why I was not able to overcome my old nature and why I struggled with the development of my inner man. It enlightened me as to why Ephesians 1:3 was not happening in my life according to the new nature and heavenly access I was supposed to have as a result of being born again.

Start day #1

Start day one was the day you were first conceived in the mind and heart of God. The Bible lets us know that every human was created by God before the foundations of the world were made [Eph. 1:3-5]. It is so important to understand that when God created us in Him, we were perfect in all of our ways. As odd as this may sound, when God created us, He also built the Kingdom of God inside of each one of us, which includes the provision and potential needed for us to maintain a perfect (mature, fully equipped) state of being.

> "For those God foreknew he also predestined to be conformed to the image of his Son, that he might be the firstborn among many brothers and sisters. And those he predestined, he also called; those he called, he also justified; those he justified, he also glorified" (Rom. 8:29-30, NIV).

God predestined us with the ability to be conformed to the image of His Son, Jesus Christ. The Spirit of Truth activates, educates and empowers every Spirit-filled believer with the potential to be completely perfect and equipped through the obedience of His instructions.

The word "perfect" used to describe Lucifer (Ez. 18:5) comes from the Hebrew word *tâmıym*, which is a powerful word that means "what has or is integrity; truth, whole, spotless, mature and righteous." When Lucifer was found with iniquity, these qualities that were built in him were perverted so that the opposite is now true of him. He has no integrity; he is a liar and the father of it; he is no longer whole or complete, but lacks; he is spotted with the stain of sinful nature; he is imperfect, immature, and unrighteous.

The word "perfect" has a meaning almost identical to the word "undefiled," found in Psalms 119:1. Hence "iniquity" is the root defiler that perverts our potential to conform to the perfect image of Christ. We were all perfect at the moment of our conception in the mind of God, before the foundation of the world. Every human is originally a citizen of the Kingdom of Heaven:

> "But our citizenship is in heaven. And we eagerly await a Savior from there, the Lord Jesus Christ" (Phil. 3:20, NIV).

Start day #2

Our second start day occurred the moment our natural conception took place through our biological parents. It does not matter who you are, where you live or how you came into this world; God allowed it to happen. Whether your earthly existence was planned, unplanned, or even if you were conceived through the tragedy of incest or rape; a God who is all knowing takes man's mishaps and turns them into His perfect creations.

> "But to as many as did receive and welcome Him, He gave the authority (power, privilege, right) to become the children of God, that is, to those who believe in (adhere to, trust in, and rely on) His name who owe their birth neither to bloods nor to the will of

the flesh [that of physical impulse] nor to the will of man [that of a natural father], but to God" [They are born of God!] (John 1:12-13, AMP).

God takes man's sometimes thoughtless decision making of introducing children into this world and turns it into an opportunity to express His will on earth. Not one person on this earth is here "by mistake." Each human is designed by God with excellence and a unique purpose.

I used to wonder why I was born into the dysfunctional family in which I grew up. I asked, "Why couldn't I have been born to someone else and somewhere else?" My resentment caused me to blame many of my struggles on the family I was born into and the environments I lived in. I allowed myself to use that mentality to keep me from moving forward in life. Since I've discovered and made a decision to remove all forms of iniquity from my life, my heart has been opened to the pure love and knowledge of God and the truth of who I really am in Christ. My purpose on this earth has become clearer and my understanding of why I was born into my family has grown. Now all the negative things that happened in my past are being used in a positive way to fulfill my God-ordained purpose. Because of this I create glory to His Name.

"And we know that in all things God works for the good of those who love him, who have been called according to his purpose" (Rom. 8:28).

Start day #3

This is the day that you were physically born into this world.

Many today suffer from a lack of understanding as to why they were birthed into this world. In some cases they don't even know who their birth parents are. Still, your life is part of God's great plan and He has built into you all that you need to accomplish that plan. Every human is the unique handiwork of God. Not one person on this earth is here by mistake.

> "Though my father and mother forsake me, the LORD will receive me" (Ps. 27:10, NIV).

> "For we are God's handiwork, created in Christ Jesus to do good works, which God prepared in advance for us to do" (Eph. 2:10, NIV).

Start day #4

This is the day that one makes the vital decision to become born again.

> "Jesus answered and said to him, Truly, truly, I say to you, Unless a man is born again, he cannot see the kingdom of God. Nicodemus said to Him, How can a man be born when he is old? Can he enter the second time into his mother's womb and be born? Jesus answered, Truly, truly, I say to you, Unless a man is born of water and the Spirit, he cannot enter into the kingdom of God. That which is born of the flesh is flesh, and that which is born of the Spirit is spirit. Do not marvel that I said to you, you must be born again" (John 3:3-7).

In my opinion, this is one of the most misunderstood principles in the Bible. Many denominational and non-denominational churches have distorted how they teach it and apply it according to its original purpose.

Start day #5

The fifth start day should happen every single day:

> "Therefore, I urge you, brothers and sisters, in view of God's mercy, to offer your bodies as a living sacrifice, holy and pleasing to God—this is your true and proper worship. Do not conform to the pattern of this world, but be transformed by the renewing of your mind. Then you will be able to test and approve what God's will is—his good, pleasing and perfect will" (Rom. 12:1-2, NIV).

"If you then be risen with Christ, seek those things which are above, where Christ sits on the right hand of God. Set your affection on things above, not on things on the earth. For you died, and your life is now hidden with Christ in God" (Col. 3:1-3).

Every day—through the power of the Holy Spirit—our minds should be renewed to the patterns and instructions of the book in Heaven that is written about us. Every believer should be receiving daily the details of what is written in the book that God has authored for their lives.

In Summary:

Start day #1 – You were perfect (what has or is integrity; truth, whole, spotless, mature and righteous) without the presence or contamination of iniquity.

Start day #2 – You were physically conceived by a male sperm which doubtless contained iniquitous traits in it.

Start day #3 – You were born naturally into this world with the same condition stated in Psalms 51:5: "Behold, I was shapen in iniquity; and in sin did my mother conceive me."

Start day #4 – You decided to be born again; in Jesus' words, "You must be born again."

Start day #5 – A mandate that needs to be a daily occurrence, to renew your mind daily.

Each one of these five "start days" has to be understood in order for you to gain full power from each of them in your life. A proper understanding of day #4 gives us access to the truth of our original perfect state at day #1. Day #5 ties those two together, with the knowledge that we must continue to renew ourselves to maintain a "perfect" (mature) condition.

If day #2 and day #3 are not properly dealt with through the removal of iniquity, day #4 will have no affect and will not bring us back to day #1's predestined condition. Many born-again believers still live their lives with the iniquitized effects of days #2 and #3. They see the negative effects and just say, "Oh well, that is who I am. It must be the will of the Lord for me to be like this."

With a mindset like that, no one will be able to overcome what the Bible refers to as the "old man" or "carnal nature." If we want to experience the full benefit of being born again—not only the promise of eternal life, but also being reintroduced to the perfection of day #1—we must allow day #5 to occur every day, which will result in our becoming a "new person" or creation in Christ [Eph. 4:22-24 & 2 Cor. 5:17].

This will enable us to experience the benefits that were conceived, built in and promised through day #1. We are reintroduced and born into these Heavenly benefits through day #4, which should eventually produce a continual refreshing through day #5's renewing-of-the-mind process, as well as receiving daily instructions straight from the Kingdom of Heaven.

It is impossible to "renew our minds" properly if we don't know what to renew it *to*. Our minds must be renewed not just with the written Word of God but also the spoken Word of God. It is the spoken word that will give us the exact details of what is written in the book that God has already preordained for each life [Ps. 139:16]. The written Word found in the Bible is a wonderful and necessary general guide, yet each believer needs to know the *specific* instructions God has for their life.

Sadly, the majority of Christians today live their lives from their "day 3" experience—when they were naturally born. Even those that claim to be born again fail to understand the significance of day #1, and therefore they miss the full benefit and purpose of day #4. We were all originally created in an iniquity-free environment by an iniquity-free God that both enables and requires us to be iniquity free as a result of our born-again experience.

I am currently writing another book, along with a curriculum, called *The Mystery of the Kingdom Revealed*. This will detail the blueprint for accurate "Kingdom of God" living. It will outline the importance of removing iniquity. It will also detail how to hear the voice of God in order to build what God has preordained for your life. In the area of getting a deeper understanding of day #1's influential power, the curriculum will give clarity into the true Christ-like identity that many believers fail to understand. This curriculum and book will help you discover your specific, preordained purpose from God for your life as well as how to get pure and clear vision and direction from God.

These resources will include material that will outline the importance of documentation and its function in building a blueprint for your life. You will be led through the process of producing what I call a "Trueprint." Your *Trueprint* will contain detailed information (truth) for your life, including the uniqueness of who you are in Christ, with components that will guide you towards an accurate building process.

It was only after I undertook the process of removing iniquity from my own life that God was able to give me these ideas. The purpose is to bring awareness and lead believers through the process of removing iniquity from their lives, and, as a result, from the body of Christ.[9]

Carrying the Cross

Every single day, God's children must make the decision to "die" [1 Cor. 15:31] to their own will and obtain the will of God for their lives. This can only be accomplished when one makes a daily decision to follow the instruction of Jesus: "If anyone desires to come after Me, let him deny himself and take up his cross and follow Me" (Luke 9:23). This is a vital element to the daily renewal-

---

[9] If you are interested in this material once completed, please use my contact information at the end of this book.

of-mind process. This is exactly what Jesus did when He chose to obey the will of His Father at every step [John 5:30].

Taking up your cross is doing away with self-will and personal interests and replacing it with living for others and representing Christ to the world. Carrying your cross in essence "kills" all that stands in the way of you understanding your purpose on the earth. It allows you to walk accurately before God through Christ.

Carrying your cross comes into play when you realize that the plans you have made for your life don't quite match up with the plans that God has in His book for your life. A realization like that is not an easy one. It requires soul searching and sacrifice. It is a death to self because we often define ourselves through the plans we have for our life. This is obvious by the way we often introduce ourselves to people: "I am a doctor," or "I am a teacher," or "I am a writer." That is not who we are. It is what we do, yet that is how we define ourselves. When we ask God about His plan for our lives, and realize it is very different from what we have defined ourselves to be, the choice before us is not an easy one. We can either refuse to pick up that cross, and thus remain on the path of iniquity—failing to accomplish God's ordination for our life—or we can pick up the cross and carry it bravely, at the same time letting go of those self-made plans and programs.

> *"I have been crucified with Christ, and I live; yet no longer I, but Christ lives in me. And that life I now live in the flesh, I live by faith toward the Son of God, who loved me and gave Himself on my behalf"* (Gal. 2:20).

One encouraging concept found throughout the Bible is the principle of the seed. This principle teaches us that in order for something to live, something has to die. Jesus had to die so that we can all live and have access to God now and forever. You and I also have to die to our will so that Christ can live within us and guide us to reproduce the life that we are predestined to live.

Iniquity provides energy for self-will and all those "self" words that come with it: *self*ishness, *self*-centeredness, *self*-sufficiency. The presence of iniquity causes us to view the cross as an unnecessary burden. In reality, carrying your cross daily is one of the highest acts of mental discipline that one must capture in order to walk in the spirit. Only then can someone have success in not succumbing to the lust of the flesh [Gal. 5:16]. It is impossible to effectively carry your personal cross daily when iniquity is present.

When we fail mentally, we fail spiritually. Carrying the cross is the most effective exercise in God's "gym" that will build spiritual muscles. Even the practice of prayer—without the full understanding of carrying one's personal cross daily—is like going to the gym to *talk* about exercising but not actually *doing* the exercises.

Our days should begin with prayer, as Jesus' did. It is at this place where your mind is daily renewed—according to preordained and prewritten information about your life—so that you won't go back to the old nature you had before you were born again into the Kingdom of Heaven. The only time you are allowed lay your cross down is when you go to sleep; you need to pick it up as soon as you wake up the next morning. The mental mindset of carrying your cross, coupled with the understanding of its purpose and personal application, is a daily requirement. It is not negotiable if you desire to follow God's call on your life. Though Jesus ultimately died on a physical cross, the reality is that He carried one mentally throughout His life. He denied His own will on a daily basis. This mental bearing of the cross was eventually coupled with the wooden one that He was later given to carry and die on for all humanity.

⌘

CHAPTER SUMMARY:

- Satan has no problem with you dealing with your sin—the *fruit* or manifestation of iniquity. What he doesn't want you to deal with is the *root* of sin, which is iniquity. As long as the root is present, the fruit of it will eventually re-grow and manifest itself.

- You have the power to change the very structure of your thinking and behaviors.

- Due to iniquity, a majority of people on earth today have no idea what God has written in the book for their life.

- Satan uses the deceptive and illusive power of iniquity to deceive us and try to keep us from discovering our "true identity" in Christ. His purpose is to ensure that the contents of the book that has already been written about you from before the foundations of the earth remain hidden.

- It is impossible to "renew our minds" properly if we don't know what to renew it *to*. Our minds must be renewed not just with the written Word of God but also the spoken Word of God.

- We must understand the significance of dying to our will so that Christ can live within us and guide us to reproduce the life that we are predestined to live.

- Carrying your cross daily is one of the highest acts of mental discipline that one must capture in order to walk in the spirit.

APPLICATION:

1. Review and make sure that you understand the significance of each the five start days as they pertain to your life.

2. Take an honest inventory of your life and acknowledge all forms of sin that you know that you are guilty of. (Review the list on the link provided to see if you are guilty of doing something that you did not even realize was a sin.)

3. Research your family line. View photo albums, ask parents, siblings or anyone else who may have knowledge of your family's history (especially from your biological father, grandfather, great grandfather and great-great grandfather) to discover issues they had, such as alcoholism, drug addiction, lust, pornography, incest, or hereditary health issues.

4. Ask God to reveal to you any iniquity that was transferred to you or that you were guilty of birthing into existence in your life.

5. Document all of your findings on paper to capture a visual of them.

6. Follow the steps in "The Iniquity Removal Process" chapter to begin a new life of freedom.

Chapter 8

Iniquity and the Church

"It is possible to become acquainted with the culture of Christianity and yet not perceive the Christ of Christianity." – Julio Alvarado Jr.

The human body has an innumerable quantity of cells. Cancer is the term for a group of diseases that all have to do with cells. Cancer results when abnormal cells grow and spread very fast. Normal body cells grow and divide and know when to stop growing. Over time, they also die. Unlike normal cells, cancer cells continue to grow and divide out of control; they don't die when they're supposed to.

Cancer cells usually group or clump together to form tumors. A growing tumor can destroy the normal cells around the tumor and damage the body's healthy tissues.

The immune system is your body's defense force. The immune system has an instinctive ability to resist cancer development: however, in most cases, the immune system fails due to sophisticated strategies that the tumor cells use to evade detection. Certain viruses and unhealthy eating or life habits can also assist in causing cancer cells to multiply. A healthy body's immune system should detect cancer cells and consider them "foreign" invaders, resulting in the healthy cells killing the foreign cancerous cells.

Physically, the cellular immune system is the most important part of the immune system for the defense against cancer.

Sad to say, iniquity has the same affect on the church body that cancer has on a human body. Iniquity has been allowed to invade, grow and multiply, causing destruction within the Body of Christ—the local churches and the body of believers across the globe.

Spiritually, the blood of Jesus combined with truth from the mouth of God are the strategic and instinctive immune system that gives us access to the antidote for iniquity. It is a major part of the defense system against the effects of the "foreign" and "destructive" invader of iniquity.

In Paul's second letter to his young disciple, Timothy, two individuals were guilty of the invasion of "iniquitized" behavior. Hymeneus and Philetus perverted the truth; their actions were compared to gangrene, a form of skin cancer.

> *"Study earnestly to present yourself approved to God, a workman that does not need to be ashamed, rightly dividing the Word of Truth. But shun profane, vain babblings, for they will increase to more ungodliness. And their word will eat like gangrene; among whom are Hymeneus and Philetus, who have erred concerning the truth, saying that the resurrection is already past, and who overthrow the faith of some. Nevertheless the foundation of God stands sure, having this seal: 'The Lord knew those who are His.' And, 'Let everyone who names the name of Christ depart from iniquity!'"* (2 Tim. 2:15-19).

Two individuals strayed from the truth regarding the resurrection, which affected other believers to the point where their faith was also contaminated. This same condition exists in the church today, a fact validated by numerous differing beliefs due to a lack of agreement on many topics under the general umbrella of "Christianity." We can have two churches on the same block that don't agree on doctrine or some denominational practice; therefore, division exists amongst them as a result. Another sad extreme is when churches accommodate and justify "iniquitized" beliefs and behavior in order to keep from offending believers. In the above passage of scripture, Paul not only addressed the issue but he also called it what it was: a cancerous effect on the body of believers. Paul confronted it in a spirit of truth and righteousness. This type of necessary confrontation is rare today.

The power of the blood of Jesus is rendered impotent in ridding our lives of iniquity when our spiritual immune system is not properly working due to a lack of truth that results in ignorance and disobedience [1 John 2:16, Eph. 1:7 & 2:13, Col. 1:13-14, & 20, Heb. 6:6, 9:14 & 10:29, 1 Pet. 1:2 & 18-19, 1 John 1:7, Rev. 1:5].

As I was writing this book, I asked approximately 20 believers—the majority of whom have been Christians for over 10 years—from different churches and denominations if they would define iniquity for me, or at least explain their understanding of it. Over half of them said they didn't know at all what it meant. About six of them defined it as "sin." Two of them defined it as "secret sins of the heart." One person even defined it as "what keeps you from becoming who God wants you to be." This last individual responded with the best answer, but afterwards, couldn't explain why they responded this way and believed it to be just a lucky guess.

If you would have asked me the same question before I had an accurate understanding of iniquity, I would have also responded with, "it is just sin," or, "I really don't know." After explaining to these individuals the original Hebrew definition and the working definition used in this book, almost all of them responded with, "Wow, that makes sense," or other similar comments. Due to this revelation, some of those with whom I spoke even began examining their own lives for the presence of iniquity. Their newfound understanding of iniquity from a root word perspective empowered them to begin a process to combat iniquity in their lives.

What is the Church?

"For where God built a church, there the devil will also build a chapel." – Martin Luther

The Greek word for church is *ekklesia*, which is defined as "the calling out or called out ones." In Hebrew, it is the word *qahal*, which means "an assembly, congregation, company or multitude." Like a physical body has to be free from destructive cancer and viruses to be in the best health possible, the same principle applies to the individual believer and to the assembly of believers.

Iniquity is the main cancer or virus that contaminates the body of Christ and causes a church body to function at less than its full potential. If Jesus is the head, and there was no iniquity in Him, shouldn't the body of Christ—the called out ones, the congregation—work towards eliminating all forms and influences of iniquity?

Psalms 82 describes the true value of who we are as humans, as well as a key problem that perverts or "iniquitizes" that value. In verse 6, God states, "I have said, you are gods; and all of you are children of the Most High." Once I understood what this verse truly said about every believer that claims to be a child of God, it amazed me. The word "gods" used here is the word *elohiym* in Hebrew which is interesting in that it is the same word ascribed to God Himself [Gen. 1:1]. The capital letter "G" is always used to describe God Himself but the smaller case letter "g" is used when it refers to humanity. In the *Ancient Hebrew Lexicon*, the word *god* means "one who yokes with another."

Using the same resource, the word "yoke" is defined as "to work together through the eye of experience and knowledge." In the Hebraic and other cultures, when they would train oxen to plow a field, they always yoked an experienced ox with an inexperienced one so that the knowledge of the older ox would influence the inexperienced ox. In other words, when we gods (little g) yoke ourselves to God (big G), He will lead us with His sight, knowledge and experience. Jesus, in Matthew 11:29-30, makes reference to this yoke.

Jesus referred to himself as the "Son of Man." This term was used 89 times in the New Testament writings, which alluded to His humanity. Jesus, as a man, was also a "god" but He was yoked to the "big G" [2 Cor. 5:19], allowing God to lead Him by what He heard and saw from God the Father [John 5:19-20, 8:28].

The significance of that verse has been lost in the body of Christ. As a result, there are many who fail to understand their perfect (mature) position yoked together with God as a god. This causes the body of Christ, the church today, to be unhealthy and not function according to its purpose. The fruit that the church is bearing today is very different from the results that God originally intended.

In the following verse, we are clued into the reason why many Christians are hindered from experiencing the full essence of whom and what they were created to be:

They know not, neither will they understand; they walk on in darkness: all the foundations of the earth are out of course" (Ps. 82:5, KJV).

They lacked knowledge and understanding and therefore walked in darkness. The word "darkness" comes from the Hebrew root word *chôshek* which means: "ignorance, misery, destruction, death, sorrow, wickedness." Ignorance is the foundational cause for the conditions of destruction, misery, sorrow and even wickedness and spiritual death. These deficiencies are all rooted in iniquity, for when someone "takes the power of truth that is to be used for reproductive or creative work and uses it for vain or other improper purposes" they will doubtless fail to be yoked together with God. They will thus manifest "son of man" behaviors instead of "Son of God" behaviors.

They become a god unto themselves and begin functioning in what the Bible calls "the pride of life" (1 John 2:16). They become their own source and sustainer of life instead of functioning in the likeness and image of God—one who relies on Him as their source and sustainer of life through complete obedience, which qualifies them to be a son of God. "There is a way that seems right to a man, but the end of it is the ways of death" (Prov. 16:25).

Psalms 82:7 states, "But you shall die like men, and fall like one of the princes." As we are children of God, we should die a natural death like "sons" and not "men." The term "man" or "men" in this case doesn't refer to just the male gender. This is important to understand because all humans—male and female—are predestined to be called sons (or children) of God, according to Galatians 4:5-6 and Ephesians 1:5. We are adopted by God through receiving the spirit of adoption [Rom. 8:15], which is the same Spirit of Truth that Jesus mentioned, more commonly known as the Holy Spirit.

This same spirit is what gives the believer power to obey the written and spoken Word of God. Obedience to God has to be the true mark or goal of a child of God. To miss this mark is to fall back into mere "men" status. Dying "like men and falling like one of the princes" is a reference to Lucifer's fall from Heaven because of the iniquity that was found in him [Ez. 28:15, Luke 10:18, Eph. 2:2].

The above points are further confirmed by the following passages:

> *"The fool has said in his heart, there is no God! They acted corruptly; they have done abominable works, there is none who does good. God looked down from Heaven on the **sons of men**, to see if there were any who understood and sought God. All have gone aside, together they are filthy; there is none who does good, no, not one. Have all the workers of iniquity not known, eating up My people as they eat bread? They have not called on God" (Ps. 14:1-4 & 53:1-4).*

Hosea 4:6 is a scripture often used to illustrate the reason for the dreadful condition of the people of God—not only in the days of the prophet Hosea but also in the church and world today. Many quote only the first part of this verse: "My people are destroyed for a lack of knowledge." However, we need to read the rest of that verse and continue on through verse 8 to find the root cause of this destruction. Many have blamed the devil for the destruction and lack in their lives but the devil cannot be blamed for our ignorance. We partner with him when we reject the truth that is available to us through the Spirit of Truth, which will educate us in the process of rooting out iniquity, enabling us to live a blessed life now and forever.

> *"My people are destroyed for a lack of knowledge. Because you have rejected knowledge, I will also reject you from being priest to Me. Since you have forgotten the Law of your God, I will also forget your sons, even I. As they were increased, so they sinned against Me. I will change their glory into shame. They feed on the sin of My people, and* **they set their heart on their iniquity**" (Hosea 4:6-8).

The first verse of this same chapter states: "There is no truth, nor mercy, nor knowledge of God in the land" [Hosea 4:1]. It wasn't that truth, mercy and the knowledge of God were not available; the problem was that the people had rejected them. Why? "They set heart on their iniquity." Truth is a key ingredient in removing iniquity from one's life. It is vital to understand what truth is since God is a God of truth. Jesus also declared Himself a manifestation of truth in John 14:6: "I am the way and the truth and the life. No one comes to the Father except through me."

Truth is not a doctrine that originates from the numerous religious beliefs and denominations that claim to have cornered the market on truth. Many religions and denominations teach that all those who do not have the exact same beliefs that they do are living in error. The fact that this is happening in many religions, denominations and beliefs today is proof that iniquity is in that environment. Truth will always unite and iniquity will always bring division. Since the Godhead is united within itself, the reality is that there should only be one doctrine of belief for the entire world. That doctrine is the *doctrine of truth* that comes from the Kingdom of Heaven, which is all that Jesus talked about while He was on this earth.

Until the bride (the Church) positions her ear before the mouth of God and takes seriously her calling to discover the totality of the doctrine of the Kingdom that Jesus taught, she will continue to struggle because she is, in essence, asking God to accommodate a doctrine that is not His; He will never become a groom to that.

In his book, *Rediscovering the Kingdom*—which in my opinion is a must-read for every human alive today, especially church, government and world leaders—Dr. Myles Munroe details the result of iniquity upon the belief system of the church and the world, past and present. It is a belief system that for the most part continues to be influenced by the traditions, philosophies and self-imposed religions of man.

The Importance of Strategic and Vigilant Prayer

> *"The real power of prayer is not what you say, but is found in what you hear and see."* – Julio Alvarado Jr.

Jesus said, "Watch and pray, lest you enter into temptation. Truly the spirit is willing, but the flesh is weak" (Mark 14:38). Christians have no problem praying but they often fail to implement the "watching" part. The word "watch" here literally means, "to have your spirit or inner man to be vigilant through insight and to abide in that place of vigilance in a prepared mode."

This is similar to a guard or soldier who has positioned himself atop a tower or hill so that he can have a better view of any attempts by the enemy to overcome him and so that he can defend the place he is protecting. That "high place" for a believer is the place we are encouraged not only to seek out but also to remain in spiritually, keeping our minds there.

> *"If you then be risen with Christ,* **seek those things which are above**, *where Christ sits on the right hand of God.* **Set your affection on things above**, *not on things on the earth. For you died, and your life is now hidden with Christ in God"* (Col. 3:1-3).

Iniquity and the Church

This passage is loaded with keys that unlock the chains that keep people bound to the things of this earth. It bids us to "set our affections on things above."

The statement, "If you then be risen with Christ," reminds me of the words we use when we tell people who brought us up, who raised us as we grew up. It speaks to the importance of Christ being the one intended to "raise" us once we are born again. Though God may use other believers to help in this process early on, the only one who should be bringing us to a place of full maturity is Christ, who is represented within the Spirit of Truth.

If you allow Christ to raise you, He will tell you what you should or should not do, like any good parent. Christ desires and is assigned to be your spiritual "nanny" in your infancy stage of being a born-again believer; He then becomes your tutor and mentor as you grow and develop through stages of your spiritual life. Your decision to submit to Christ determines whether you mature into the image of a son of God. You must first provide the environment of obedience towards Him in your heart.

Your decision to follow His guidance will give you the ability of being able to "seek those things above," since the Holy Spirit is the only guide authorized to give you the truth that God desires to show you.

> "Howbeit when he, the Spirit of Truth, is come, he will guide you into all truth: for he shall not speak of himself; but whatsoever he shall hear, that shall he speak: and he will shew you things to come" (John 16:13, KJV).

The iniquity found within Lucifer caused him to be kicked out of Heaven. As Heaven is free of iniquity, if we continue to allow iniquity to manifest itself in our lives, it is impossible to "seek those things above," much less keep our minds there. Iniquity keeps God's children from a pure and unhindered relationship with Him.

The Spirit of Truth delivers pure, undefiled knowledge straight from God. This knowledge is power. It comes in the form of instructions and illustrations that we are supposed to follow in order to create and reproduce what is predestined for us to do.

> *"For we are His workmanship, created in Christ Jesus to good works, which God has before ordained that we should walk in them" (Eph. 2:10).*

> *"Who has saved us and called us with a holy calling, not according to our works, but according to His own purpose and grace which was given us in Christ Jesus before the eternal times" (2 Tim. 1:9).*

Paul addressed the body of believers in Ephesus, saying that it is possible to be a "believer" but still not be learning from Christ Himself. These same words apply to believers today:

> *"But you have not so learned Christ, if indeed you have heard Him and were taught by Him, as the truth is in Jesus. For you ought to put off the old man (according to your way of living before) who is corrupt according to the deceitful lusts, and be renewed in the spirit of your mind. And you should put on the new man, who according to God was created in righteousness and true holiness" (Eph. 4:20-24).*

Because we in the church have lost the art of watching, many in the church—including me—have been guilty of praying for the wrong things. We, in essence, try to turn God into a Santa Clause, claiming, "I've been so good, God, you should give me the requests and gifts that I am asking for." Or perhaps we view God as a genie; if you rub Him the right way, He will grant you all that you wish for.

When Jesus instructs us to "watch," He provides what we need to do so. The Spirit of Truth gives us an inner awareness into what we should be praying for. Two "inner senses" are built into the heart of human beings and we are supposed to be aware of and develop them. We are given *inner eyes*, which provide insight to what God desires to show us; we also have *inner ears*, which enable us to receive verbal instructions from God through the Spirit of Truth [John 16:13].

> "This is why I speak to them in parables. Though seeing, they do not see; though hearing, they do not hear or understand. In them is fulfilled the prophecy of Isaiah: 'You will be ever hearing but never understanding; you will be ever seeing but never perceiving. For this people's heart has become calloused; they hardly hear with their ears, and they have closed their eyes. Otherwise they might see with their eyes, hear with their ears, understand with their hearts and turn, and I would heal them.' But blessed are your eyes because they see, and your ears because they hear" (Matt. 13:13-16, NIV).

God designed life to be lived from the inside out. This was Jesus' process of living and functioning while on this earth, it needs to be ours as well. Jesus' life was lived from the inside out in that the Kingdom of God within was exposed to Him through the inner senses—the spiritual eyes and ears that were fully developed and functional within Him.

Many Christians today continue to live their lives from the outside in; they allow the senses of their physical ears and eyes to be the main portals of information they use to live their lives. This is why many Christians suffer from fear, anxiety, insecurity and many other negative things. They allow the events and influences of the world to plot their course of living instead of allowing the Holy Spirit to influence their worldview and decision-making process [John 17:14, Eph. 1:3-5, Phil. 3:20, 1 Cor. 15:45-50].

Many churches today mention the inner man and even touch on the importance of its development. However, they often fail to go into detail of what this process should look like. The next book I'm developing in this series teaches this important process. The working title is: *Prayer—How to Hear and See like Jesus*. The church does a great job giving *knowledge of* God, yet in many cases still lacks in instructing Christians how to *know* God on a more intimate level through the development of the *inner ears* and *inner eyes* of the spirit.

Many churches major on the importance of the believer living a life of prosperity through the external evidences of finances, property and other material things. However, the first thing we must allow to grow and prosper is the inner man. We must get to the stage of maturity where we are developed in the wisdom and stature of Christ [Luke 2:42 & 8:14, Eph. 3:16 & 4:13, Col. 1:8, Philem. 1:6].

God is only obligated to prosper your life according the purpose or assignment that He has given you. Once the Spirit of Truth is allowed to develop and strengthen the inner man without the hindrance of iniquity, the inner man will prosper in knowledge and understanding. The application of that knowledge becomes the Wisdom of God for you that leads you to follow God's plan for your life. Then and only then can you discover what prosperity and inheritance you have access to and the right to claim; it will always be in proportion to the unique purpose that God has preordained for you.

What is Faith?

"Authentic faith is conceived in what God tells you and shows you, not in what you have the ability to believe." – Julio Alvarado Jr.

When Jesus lived on this earth, He lived by faith. He believed and trusted in what He saw and heard through the spiritual senses of His inner eyes and inner ears. It was this spiritual sight and hearing that fed His inner mind as well as His emotions and will. It gave Him the strength to be in control of all the situations He encountered, including the scourging and crucifixion.

Initially, every believer starts off by just believing in salvation through Jesus and in the Bible, which I call "new believer blind and deaf faith." The maturing process comes through developing the inner man [Eph. 3:16]. Every believer needs to develop their inner eyes and ears, which happens through the training and guidance of the Spirit of Truth. The written Word of God, coupled with the spoken Word of God, are the only things that that we are supposed to have faith in. Hebrews 11: 6 informs us that it is impossible to please God without having faith. God ultimately desires for us to have not just a blind faith in Him and His Word; He desires for us to have a faith that sees and hears the details of the instructions that He will give us if we are tuning in to Him.

Faith that is not genuinely God-inspired will eventually disappear or, worse yet, be manipulated through one's attempt to bring something to pass that is not according to God's perfect plan. Real faith at first is invisible to our natural eyes, yet it can be seen or made visible through the inner eyes. This is the kind of faith that is turned into clear and attainable vision, which should be accompanied with a strategic plan in order to fulfill it. Second Corinthians 5:7 states that we are supposed to "walk by faith and not by sight." The word "sight" here refers to what is seen through our physical eyes. We are to walk or live by the faith that comes from the words that we hear from God. These words must be converted into literal images of vision that now become supernatural insight seen through the inner eyes that our natural sense of sight cannot attain until it is manifested.

Faith is the currency that is meant to be exchanged between the Kingdom of Heaven, where all faith should originate, and the Kingdom of God that lies within every human being. Paper currency or money has no value in itself, only the value that man says it is worth. Faith by itself has no value unless it is activated by the works (Eph. 2:10) that God predestined and created you to do.

Faith is the power of belief that comes through the eyes and ears of heavenly insight. However, it will remain out of sight if iniquity is allowed to have its way. Once again, it's important to remember that Jesus walked and lived by faith, not by what He heard and saw in the natural. This kind of living is foreign to many in the church and the world today. I used to be one of them. Iniquity has rendered true faith impotent by reducing it into wishful thinking and selfish ambitions.

"So then faith comes by hearing, and hearing by the word of God" (Rom. 10:17, NKJV).

"Word" in this passage is the word *rhēma* in the Greek language. It means "an utterance through speech." In Hebrew, the root word is *emet*, which means "something said." If we are faithful to listen to the voice of God, we will discover what we are to have faith in and for.

In Hebrews 11, often called The Hall of Faith, we read of numerous men and women who received promises by faith through the instructions they received from God, not from their own desires or will—which would have been impure and iniquitized.

> *"These all died by way of faith, not having received the promises, but **having seen them afar off**. And they were persuaded of them and embraced them and confessed that they were strangers and pilgrims on the earth"* (Heb. 11:13).

These great patriarchs understood that their faith and sight did not come from the current world that they lived in, but from Heaven.

Even the Bible definition of faith tells us that faith is tangible through the eyes (inner) that hope for something from God. If something is seen through the natural eyes, it can no longer be hoped for, since it is already present. Yet what is seen internally is the evidence of the things not yet seen externally. The amazing fact is that the things "unseen" are actually more real because they originate from God and already exist in His predestined, perfect will.

> *"Now faith is the substance of things hoped for, the evidence of things not seen"* (Heb. 11:1).

Now just because I have the power to believe in something does not mean that I should have faith for it. This is the danger with many of the prosperity messages that are being taught today. Anything beyond faith *from God* is simply wishful thinking; it could be nothing more than selfish desires and ambitions. Iniquity is the culprit that produces such thinking and desires.

Faith that is blind and deaf is susceptible to pitfalls and may lead to manmade attempts to fabricate something that God never planned for your life. However, when you attach inner eyes to what God has spoken or shown you, your faith is no longer blind. This is what the Bible refers to as "vision." Vision is the manifestation of your purpose through internal images from God that work as a visual guide for you to fulfill your predestined assignment. We are supposed to experience God-given vision every day of our lives.

James 2:14-22 tells us that faith without works is dead. The word "works" is the Greek word *ergon*: "what one is supposed to be occupied with." This same word is rooted in the Hebrew word *melâ'kâh*: "deputyship that is ministry." Deputyship means "what one is delegated or assigned to do." The works that James calls us to employ, occupy and eventually deploy are the works assigned to us from God: you need to be occupied with the service or delegated assignment that is your specific purpose.

God will provide all our needs. This is a biblical promise and one we can definitely claim. He will provide that which we need to fulfill His purposes on this earth. Healing is one of the benefits that we have access to through the written and spoken Word of God. We have the power to see and experience its manifestation as a result of being a citizen of the Kingdom of Heaven. "But our citizenship is in heaven" (Phil. 3:20a, NIV).

The main reason why God heals us is so that we can complete our purpose on this earth. Even when we are the cause of our unhealthiness, God still can show His goodness through physical and mental healing. However, if our primary focus is to cast away the works of iniquity in our lives, we will automatically be obeying God's laws for healthy living and thereby have full faith to claim His healing in our lives. We can also have the faith that if He allows a sickness or some physical ailment to affect us, it must be part of His perfect plan—and will in some way be utilized to enable us to fulfill our purpose on earth.

Purposed?

> "When someone's purpose is found in any other place other than the mouth of God, their life has the potential to demonstrate the most tragic form of abuse." – Julio Alvarado Jr.

Pastor Rick Warren of Saddleback Church in Lake Forest, California, wrote a book titled *The Purpose Driven Life*.[10] Since its publication in 2007, an estimated 52 million copies of the book have been sold. The theme of his book dealt with the question, "Why am I here on the earth today?" This is a question that every single one of us, at some point in our lives, asks ourselves. It is our heart's cry. Each one of us desires to discover the inherent purpose that God has placed inside of every human being.

The question of "Why am I here?" automatically lends itself to other questions such as, "Who am I?" or "What was I born to do?" and "Where is my place in life?" A deep craving of every human spirit is to find a sense of significance and relevance.

The high numbers of sales of this book and others like it speak to the fact that people are searching for a deeper meaning to their life. Purpose is defined as, "The reason for which something is done or created or for which something exists." Purpose is the primary key to finding meaning in life. We can know that we are purposed through promises given in the Bible:

> "In whom also we have been chosen to an inheritance, being predestinated according to the purpose of Him who works all things according to the counsel of His own will" (Eph 1:11).

> "And we know that all things work together for good to those who love God, to those who are called according to His purpose" (Rom. 8:28).

---

[10] www.christianpost.com/news/rick-warren-embarks-on-follow-up-to-purpose-driven-life-39893/

The discovery of our individual and unique purpose is so important because it leads to knowing how we should function in life. It is the discovery of how you are called to become an answer to a world problem. It brings awareness to your specific assignment in life.

The discovery of your purpose is the doorway that leads to the gifts, talents and abilities that you must first discover, and then develop and deploy into the world. In essence, the discovery of your purpose is the discovery of the uniqueness of "The Real You." It allows you to be yourself.

Without the accurate discovery of original purpose, life ends up being nothing more than an experiment. It often turns into a chaotic journey that is consistently filled with frustration, disappointments and a multitude of failures. My personal life modeled this pattern for many years, even after I became a believer.

Without purpose, life seems to almost be instinctively filled with "trial and error" living, influenced by our immediate environment and the circumstances of the moment. Life has no sense of true direction or precision. The lack of purpose in one's life will lead them to imitate someone else or to invent their own purpose.

Though *The Purpose Driven Life* and books similar to it contain great content and speak to the universal need of discovering one's purpose, many who read these books are still experiencing emptiness and lack of fulfillment. They have yet to discover their original preordained purpose, which may be due to the fact that that the cancer of iniquity is present in their lives.

Whenever your purpose is not known, misuse and abuse of one's life is inevitable. The purpose of a thing is always found in the mind of the one who created it. Real authentic purpose for your life is found in the mouth of God. God is the author of purpose, and if we want to hear God and allow Him to reveal our purpose, we must rid our lives of iniquity in order to have the freedom to discover and live out a truly "purpose-driven" life.

According to the Will of God

> *"This is the confidence we have in approaching God: that if we ask anything according to his will, he hears us. And if we know that he hears us—whatever we ask—we know that we have what we asked of him" (1 John 5:14-15).*

The word "will" in this passage means, "a decreed purpose or desire." I have the right to ask God for anything I need that is related to the decreed purpose for my life. This is what I can have faith to ask for.

> *"For we are God's workmanship, created in Christ Jesus to do good works, which God prepared in advance for us to do" (Eph. 2:10).*

The good works that we are meant to do are the ones that have been prepared in advance for us to accomplish. We will receive this information only from the Spirit of Truth.

Iniquity has perverted the crucial understanding of pure faith. This is why many find themselves begging God for things that they claim to have the faith for, but begging doesn't cause God to react. God is only obligated to release what He has "prepared in advance."

Many, including myself, use the writings of the prophet in the book of Habakkuk to teach the importance of hearing the voice of God in order to receive an accurate vision for one's life.

When Habakkuk wrote the following passage, he had gotten to a point in his life where there were many problems. These issues were corrupting life and he needed an answer from God in order to understand what part he needed to play in correcting the situation he faced.

> *"I will stand upon my watch, and set me upon the tower, and will watch to see what he will say unto me, and what I shall answer when I am reproved. And the LORD answered me, and said, 'Write the vision, and make it plain upon tables, that he may run that readeth it. For the vision is yet for an appointed time, but at the*

end it shall speak, and not lie: though it tarry, wait for it; because it will surely come, it will not tarry. Behold, his soul which is lifted up is not upright in him: but the just shall live by his faith'" (Hab. 2:1-4, KJV).

Each one of us is created by God to be an answer to a problem on this earth. Could you imagine what this world would be like if everyone would discover this for their life and become that answer? Habakkuk's experience in these passages clues us in to not only the discovery of what answer to the world we are meant to be, but also the importance of faith in this process.

Habakkuk got his faith and direction for this situation from what he heard and saw from God, causing him to be "just." The word "just" in this verse is a very powerful word. In Hebrew, it is *tsaddıyq*, which means "one who is lawful, righteous, straight or upright." This is the root word for the common English word "justice." In other words, when God gives you a word of instruction or a vision, it literally becomes a law unto you. Your obedience to fulfill that instruction causes you to be justified in righteousness and uprightness before God.

Verse four is vital in understanding how iniquity infects the voice and insight of God. When it speaks of "his soul which was lifted up," this defines what pride does to a person. Pride is defined as, "Self confidence, one who trusts in his own resources and power, to be self existent." The pride of life is one of the three doorways where sin is birthed into one's life [1 John 2:16]. When pride enters a life, it inflates the soul to a position that says "I don't need God; I can be a god unto myself."

Pride was a manifestation of the iniquity that Lucifer had [Ez. 28:5, 17, 31:10]. This type of pride will even affect how one prays to God. Our prayers need to be according to the pure will of God and not the "iniquitized" will of man. A perfect example of this was Jesus praying in the garden of Gethsemane. He was sorely tempted to follow the path of iniquity rather than take the cup that was set before Him, a cup that he knew was filled with pain, anguish and suffering. He pleaded to His Father, "If thou be willing, remove this cup from me." Then He went on to accept the perfect plan of the Father, once again overcoming the temptation of iniquity upon His life, when He said, "Yet not My will, but Yours be done" (Luke 22:42).

The following passage instructs us that we should pray for things that are related to will of God and not our will. Many believers' prayers today are self centered; they focus more on personal wants and needs rather than the will of God.

> *"And this is the confidence that we have toward Him, that if we ask anything **according to His will**, He hears us"* (1 John 5:14).

As we pray and are open to the whispers of the Holy Spirit of Truth, He will deliver spiritual insight to us. The information He gives us is that which we have the right to pray for because it lines up with His Word and His will.

> *"Howbeit when he, the Spirit of Truth, is come, he will guide you into all truth: for he shall not speak of himself; but whatsoever he shall hear, that shall he speak: and he will shew you things to come. He shall glorify me: for he shall receive of mine, and shall shew it unto you"* (John 16:13-14, KJV).

The Greek word *shew* means "to show, rehearse, to announce in detail." This word is rooted in the Hebrew word *châzâh*, which means "to mentally gaze at or perceive, to see or have vision for." What is interesting about both the Greek and Hebrew definitions is that, when they are combined, we can conclude that what the Holy Spirit shows us is that the vision we are to mentally perceive (or gaze to stare at) through the sense of the inner eyes is something that has already been done in the mind of God.

This vision is announced through detailed words and/or images by the Holy Spirit rehearsing to you what has already taken place in the heart of God for your life. This is similar to an actor getting a script from an original writer for a part they are about to portray in a motion picture. The script will contain *words* that the actor must repeat as well as details of the *scenes* in which the episode will take place in. The script equips the actor with foreknowledge and visualization. In actuality the actor is given a glimpse of the future before it comes to pass.

The *Ancient Hebrew Lexicon of the Bible* also defines *châzâh* as: "To have the ability to see beyond what is seen, as light piercing through darkness." In Hebrew thought, light is always a reference to knowledge and darkness is a reference to ignorance or lack of knowledge. John 1:4 states, "In him was life; and the life was the light of men." True life is found in knowledge of the truth. Jesus was truth walking on two feet; you and I have to be truth walking on two feet as well. Truth is the purest form of light or knowledge and it has the power to expose and eliminate any form of darkness or lack of knowledge in one's life.

> "And this is the message which we have heard from Him and declare to you, that God is light, and in Him is no darkness at all. If we say that we have fellowship with Him and walk in darkness, we lie and do not practice the truth. But if we walk in the light, as He is in the light, we have fellowship with one another, and the blood of Jesus Christ His Son cleanses us from all sin" (1 John 1:5-7).

Many believers today walk in ignorance in crucial areas such as understanding their true preordained identity, purpose, vision and mission. Due to this ignorance, they fail to pray accurately. What is interesting is that a study of Jesus' prayer life shows that He never prayed for the things that many believers pray for. Jesus, who is our model, only prayed along the lines of His Father's known will for His life.

The Importance of Vision to the Congregation

> *"It is a terrible thing to see and have no vision. The only worse thing than being blind is having sight but no vision."* – Helen Keller

Jesus was very skilled in the practice of vision. As He saw His Father do, He did likewise. Jesus was the biggest imitator that the world has ever known, yet this is the practice of vision in its purest and most accurate form. This is the process that we all need to follow.

> 'Then Jesus answered and said to them, 'Truly, truly, I say to you, The Son can do nothing of Himself but what He sees the Father do. For whatever things He does, these also the Son does likewise'" (John 5:19-20).

We often overlook this vital process because we mentally put Jesus on a pedestal of spirituality. We assume we can never attain this type of praying. However, Romans 8:29 states: "For those God foreknew he also predestined to be conformed to the image of his Son, that he might be the firstborn among many brothers and sisters."

Every human is foreknown by God. Because of this, everyone is predestined by God with the ability to be conformed (to be similar or fashioned like) to the image of God's Son, Jesus. Jesus is the "firstborn among many brothers and sisters." This is one of the main reasons that it is important to understand the true purpose and application of the born-again experience. Jesus was naturally the firstborn on this earth from God, the Father—the original source of life. We are those who are born after Jesus through the born-again experience. Becoming born again gives us access to Heaven for all that we need to enable us to fulfill our purpose on this earth. One of these abilities is that we have the power to see and hear like Jesus did, internally [Col. 3:1-3 and Phil. 4:19].

I used to wonder who or what was Jesus seeing when He said, "The Son can do nothing of Himself but what He sees the Father do. For whatever things He does, these also the Son does likewise" (John 5:19).

If God is a Spirit, what image was Jesus seeing? John 1:18 makes it clear that no one has seen God at any time and that Jesus only

Iniquity and the Church

declared the Father. Remember that Jesus was functioning as a human, just like me and you, on this earth.

Below are some scriptures that I believe solve this mystery and give us insight into the unadulterated process of true vision understanding and application.

> "I speak what I have seen with My Father, and you, then, do what you have seen with your father" (John 8:38).

> "I and the Father are one!" (John 10:30)

> "If you had known Me, you would have known My Father also. And from now on you know Him and have seen Him" (John 14:7).

> "Jesus said to him, Have I been with you such a long time and yet you have not known Me, Philip? He who has seen Me has seen the Father. And how do you say, Show us the Father?" (John 14:9)

> "Whereas God was in Christ reconciling the world to Himself, not imputing their trespasses to them, and putting the word of reconciliation in us" (2 Cor. 5:19).

Jesus saw *Himself* when He said "The Son can do nothing of Himself but what He sees the Father do. For whatever things He does, these also the Son does likewise" (John 5:19).

This is vision in its purest state. We all need this same vision, but the presence of iniquity will pervert the vital process of hearing, seeing, saying, and doing like Jesus did. Iniquity exchanges this power for manmade wishing, which many today mistake for vision.

When you are pursuing God's vision for your life, the question that needs to be addressed is, "What do I see myself doing according to the words and visualization that the Spirit of Truth provides?" If you are a pastor or leader of any kind, this is the question you must ask first for yourself and then for your congregation. The Holy Spirit produces the vision by depositing information and insight into one's mind. This insight is based on predestined events that God has already seen done before we even do them.

Many believers today have no vision for their lives. For the first 15 years of my Christian walk, I didn't either because of ignorance rooted in iniquity. It wasn't until I began the iniquity removal process that the Holy Spirit was able to begin showing me what my original purpose was, which led me to get the vision for my life.

There are many today that know their purpose and have a vision for their lives, but the presence and practice of iniquity delays the process and in some cases causes the unfortunate death of that purpose and vision for their lives.

Iniquity is the #1 Kingdom of God killer. Jesus, when questioned by the religious Pharisees of His day as to when the Kingdom of God would come, said that the Kingdom of God is within us [Luke 17:20-21]. Paul was inspired by God to give us the three main components of this Kingdom of God within us: righteousness, peace and joy in the Holy Spirit [Rom. 14:17]. One cannot be righteous without truth, much less experience the pure peace and joy of God. Truth is the foundation of righteousness. Iniquity introduces falseness into our lives; it darkens and distorts the reality of who we truly are. This in turn keeps us from being upright before God and experiencing true peace, which only comes through operating from a whole, complete, fully-equipped position in life. God and the believer both experience true joy when His creations are walking in their predestined authority and purpose. Every spirit-filled believer has access to this iniquity-free, "Kingdom of God" manifestation.

In order for a church to be healthy, it must be populated with healthy people. I'm not referring to physical health, but spiritual health. Every believer has to get to the place where they are walking in the fullness of God's intended will, absent from the Kingdom-of-God-killer virus of iniquity.

Many born-again believers get delivered from the *environments* of their past yet sadly never allow themselves to be set free from their negative *effects*. So many Christians know and quote scripture and claim all the promises of God, yet they still can't seem to overcome negative thinking or behaviors. They are emotionally depressed or mentally oppressed; in many cases they live undisciplined lives and face deficiency in many areas. They are faithful to attend church, give tithes and offerings and even minister in different capacities, yet still don't experience the promises of God in their lives.

I was one of them. I dealt with all the above in a fatalistic fashion. From time to time I would sadly say, "Oh well, it must be the will of the Lord for me to be like this," and reconcile myself to my sad fate. All the while, I had the power to free myself from these chains of bondage. It was available to me, as it is to every believer, through the absorption of the Spirit of Truth in every area of my life.

If the church would come to a full understanding of iniquity and enlighten believers on the topic, if each member of the body of Christ would take responsibility and root out iniquity from his or her life, the church would be strengthened and able to finally start moving forward in the way that God originally intended. God would truly be seen for what He is—our refuge and strength, and a very present help in the midst of the world's trouble [Psalm 46:1]. Not only that, but we would have the power to stand against the tide of evil in the world today and be a voice for truth, and a shining light in the midst of growing darkness.

The "God" Kind of Love

The Bible says that God is love [1 John 4:8]. The word love in this verse is commonly translated from the Greek language as *agape*, which many translate as "the God-kind of love." The original word in Hebrew is *ahav*, which means "the father revealed." Since the nature of God is love, wouldn't it be safe to say that every believer that claims to have God in their lives should be revealing this same nature?

I hear many excuses as to why the church is in the condition that it is today. It is not only because people aren't praying or reading the

Bible enough; it is also because Satan has been allowed to disable the body of Christ through the same thing that disconnected him from the presence of God: iniquity.

Instead of being a place where God's power of love is expressed in a life-changing manner, the church in many cases has become a place of impotence. Rather than producing life, love and hope, it adds to the failure of much of the world today.

I want make it clear that my intention is not to be critical towards the church. God intended for the church to be the most powerful and influential organization on the earth. In no way is this book intended to speak negatively about any denomination or belief. As mentioned earlier, this book is not purposed to *offend* anyone, but to *defend* them by helping them to discover and eliminate any form of iniquity in their lives.

We—individually as believers, and collectively as the body of Christ—have the power to expose Satan's use and power of iniquity. It is no longer a mystery ... and now—while the gift of God's mercy and grace through His truth is still available—we can do our part to spread the message of the Kingdom of God through the genuine love and favor of God. He has given us access to forgiveness of sins and iniquities and will restore us back to the powerful predestined people that we are purposed to be.

> *"For the mystery of iniquity doth already work: only he who now letteth will let, until he be taken out of the way. And then shall that Wicked be revealed, whom the Lord shall consume with the spirit of his mouth, and shall destroy with the brightness of his coming"* (2 Thess. 2:7-8, KJV).

⌘

Chapter Summary:

- ***Iniquity is the cancerous "foreign" invader that*** has been allowed to invade, grow and multiply, causing destruction within the Body of Christ—the local churches and the body of believers across the globe. It has caused the church body to function at less than its full potential.

- Truth will always unite and iniquity will always bring division.

- The Godhead is united within itself; therefore, there should only be one doctrine of belief for the entire world: the doctrine of The Kingdom of God that originated from the mouth of God.

- When Jesus instructs us to "watch," He provides what we need to do so. The Spirit of Truth gives us an inner awareness into what we should be watching and praying for.

- Life is designed by God to be lived from the inside out.

- Faith is the currency that is exchanged between the Kingdom of Heaven—where all faith should originate from—and the Kingdom of God that is within every human.

- Just because I have the power to believe in something does not mean that I should have faith for it.

- A deep craving of every human spirit is to find a sense of significance and relevance. Purpose is the primary key to finding meaning in life.

- The discovery of your purpose is the discovery of the uniqueness of "The Real You." Without the accurate discovery of original purpose, life ends up being nothing more than an experiment.

- Real, authentic purpose for your life is found in the mouth of God.

- The presence of iniquity will pervert the vital process of hearing, seeing, saying and doing like Jesus did. This is vision displayed in its purest state.

- In order for a church to be healthy, it must be populated with spiritually healthy people.

- Many born-again believers get delivered from the *environments* of their past yet sadly never allow themselves to be set free from the negative *effects* of their past.

APPLICATION:

1. Think about your perception of topics such as purpose, vision, faith, healing and prayer. Considering what you just learned, do you need to re-examine these areas in your belief and practice so that you can more accurately experience inner growth and development in your life?

2. We have discovered that Jesus is the head of the church, and there was and is no iniquity in Him. It is vital to understand that the responsibility therefore falls on the "called out ones," the congregation, to work towards eliminating all forms and influences of iniquity. Take some time to reflect on your church and/or ministry experiences. Can you see where iniquity might be present? Document these findings and make prayerful plans to rid these areas of iniquity.

Chapter 9

Iniquity Within the Family Unit

"The family is one of God's strongest foundational structures and yet it is so easily fractured." – Julio Alvarado Jr.

Just as iniquity can affect each member of the church overall, so it has the potential to affect each member within a family unit. Clearly, every member of the body of Christ has a unique part to play and their commitment to playing that part determines the effectiveness of the church overall. Likewise, on a smaller scale, the family unit has a unique role to play. Their faithfulness to play that part, or their failure to do so, affects the family to a greater degree than we may care to admit.

Considering some current statistics on families across America, and throughout the world, something is not as it should be in regard to the family structure. Eleven countries have a divorce rate of *over* 50%, meaning that, if trends continue, over half of all marriages in those countries will end up in divorce. The United States has a divorce rate of 49%. Seven additional countries have a divorce rate somewhere between 40 and 49 percent.[11]

More children are being raised in one-parent families than ever before in history. Across the United States, five states reported that 40 to 50 percent of children are being raised in single-parent households. Thirty-three states report that 30 to 40 percent of children are being raised by one parent. The overall percentage

---
[11] "Worldwide Divorce Statistics." Divorce.com. 2012. Accessed 21 Apr. 2012.

is that 34% of children across the US are being reared in a single-parent family.[12]

Half a century ago, we might have been able to make the observation that the integrity of the family unit is at risk. Today, it has all but completely fallen apart. Family members have forgotten their roles. Even if they know what their roles are and wish that they could play them, the dynamics of the world today make it nearly impossible for them to do so.

Before we get further, a clarification is needed to make it clear that no single gender is completely to blame in the problems we are facing in the family structure. It is due to the effects of iniquity, which play out differently in each life, and more generally by gender, causing widespread effects for the family unit as a whole. While I'm not going to delve into specific issues, I believe that every human being should have the opportunity to express themselves and stand on an even plane when it comes to rights; at the same time, each one does bear different responsibilities due to their gifts and callings.

The Bible says that the gifts and callings of God are without repentance [Rom 11:29], making it clear that He does give specific callings to individuals and bestows upon them the gifts they need to fulfill those callings. Following His plan leads to blessings and the fulfillment of His perfect purpose, which will further the Kingdom of Heaven on Earth. Failure to follow His plan is borne of iniquity and leads to sin—missing the mark of His instructions.

So how does iniquity come into play within the family structure? The following observations and instances are only a small sampling, yet should serve to give an overall picture of the effects of iniquity within families.

---

[12] "Children in Single-Parent Families." Data Across States. The Annie E. Casey Foundation. Kids Count Data Center. 2012. Accessed 24 Apr. 2012.

Creating and Comforting

The woman has a unique role, one that no man can play. It is a role that is, in some ways, closer to God's role than anything else. Only within a woman's womb can a new life be created and formed. God does the creation and forming, but He needs a place to do it, and He has chosen the sacred place of a woman's womb to form His most glorious creation: a human life.

> *The most important person on earth is a mother. She cannot claim the honor of having built Notre Dame Cathedral. She need not. She has built something more magnificent than any cathedral—a dwelling for an immortal soul, the tiny perfection of her baby's body . . . The angels have not been blessed with such a grace. They cannot share in God's creative miracle to bring new saints to Heaven. Only a human mother can. Mothers are closer to God the Creator than any other creature; God joins forces with mothers in performing this act of creation . . . What on God's good earth is more glorious than this: to be a mother?*[13]

The woman's role is one of creating, nurturing and comforting. It is a God-given gift as well as responsibility. Someone might consider this stereotyping a woman into a subservient role; yet consider for a moment the following scenario.

Someone has a problem and goes to a male friend about it. He will doubtless come up with a solution to the issue. If there is a problem, there must be a solution and men are naturally good at filling a "fix-it" role.

A woman, however, will have a different response. She will listen to the problem. She will sympathize and often empathize as well, understanding that listening and sympathizing are every bit as supportive as—if not more so than—coming up with a quick "fix-it" to the issue. This comforting and supportive nature gives the person facing a problem the assurance that they are accepted

---

[13] Mindszenty, Joseph Cardinal. *Life Before Life.* Author: Sarah Hinze. Cedar Fort: 1993.

and loved, and that someone is concerned for them. Their ability increases to then create a solution and find the answers to the problem, whether it is an emotional issue or a practical or spiritual one. The problem may not be solved in a day, but when someone—whether a child or an adult—knows they can go to a woman, who is the picture of support, concern and empathy for as long as is needed, they will eventually make it through that time of difficulty.

In the traditional or average two-parent family—which as the statistics at the beginning of this chapter show is growing more rare—if a child has a problem with a broken toy, she will most likely go to daddy to fix it. If a blossoming teenager has a problem with a broken heart, she's going to go to her mom, not because she thinks it's going to be fixed in a day, but because that comfort and nurturing is almost more important than the problem being completely fixed. Just knowing that someone understands, and has walked those shoes and can give that promise that "It's going to be okay," makes all the difference in the world.

Some men do have the ability to listen and empathize. Some women tend towards a more "fix-it" personality, yet the general tendency of women and men, which is affirmed in a variety of studies, is for the woman to be more inclined to listen and support and for the man to be more solution oriented. "Research has revealed that in mixed-sex conversations, men interrupt women far more than the other way around. Men are also more likely than women to use judgmental adjectives. Differences like these show that men's speech is characteristically more direct, succinct and task-oriented. By contrast, women's speech is more typically indirect, elaborate, and focused on relationships. Women typically use statements showing support for the other person. Traditionally, female speech often contains statements of sympathy and empathy.[14]

Just as God gives particular callings to individuals, He also gives general callings to genders as a whole. This is not to say that only the man can or should be the breadwinner. Perhaps a mother

---

[14] Adler, B. Ronald and Russell F. Proctor. *Looking Out, Looking In*. 13th Edition. Cengage Learning. 2011.

wishes she could be there to nurture her children and raise them right, but because of the economy, her husband suffered a cut back in pay or hours or lost his job altogether and she must also get a job outside the home to bring in what is needed for them to survive.

Sometimes a husband has passed away, or lost his job, or is not as well educated as the wife. Sometimes there is no father, and the mother has to play two full-time roles, that of a mother and a "father." Obviously, the members of a family have to do what they need to survive and to have all that they need. Yet even when these other factors come into play, the woman must still make a decision whether to strive to fulfill her particular plan and purpose, or whether to let the tide of the world keep her from doing that which God has ordained for her life.

Meant to be Courageous

Many women in the church today can be heard to say something to the effect of, "I would be more than happy to play *my* God-given role, if only my husband would play *his* as father and spiritual leader of this household." Some men are excellent providers and do their best to make sure that their families are well taken care of when it comes to their wants and needs. A man can provide for his family in a variety of ways: with food, shelter, finances, clothing, protection, education, vacations and many other basic needs and wants. However, if he fails to provide for them *spiritually*, he has failed to provide the most important foundation that the family structure needs.

It would not be an exaggeration to state that the majority of problems in the church and, in fact, the world at large, are due to the male not functioning according to God's original design. Throughout history, within most societies, men have been the ones to make decisions—small or great—and we can see the sad effects of these decisions throughout the earth.[15]

These tragic effects play out personally in the lives of the women and children. There are numerous examples in the Bible of women and children who were drastically affected by the husband or male leader of the family due to his iniquitized behavior.

One such instance occurred not long after the Israelites made their exodus from Egypt. The story is found in Numbers, Chapter 16. Three men—Korah, Dathan and Abiram—approached Moses, accusing him of exalting himself above the rest of the people. Moses responded by saying that *God* would make it clear who *He* had chosen to lead the people. He told them to come back the next morning with their censers burning, and "the one whom He chooses He will cause to come near to Him" (Num. 16:5).

The next morning, "Korah gathered all the congregation against them at the door of the tabernacle of meeting" (Num. 16:19). They didn't have to wait long for God's response. The glory of the Lord appeared and He told Aaron and Moses to step aside while He consumed the entire congregation with fire. The two godly men pleaded, "Shall one man sin, and You be angry with all the congregation?" (Num. 16:22)

The Lord then told Moses to get everyone away from the tents of Dathan, Abiram and Korah. The congregation did as they were told, as the three iniquitous men stood at the doors of their tents, their wives and children standing beside them.

> "And Moses said: 'By this you shall know that the LORD has sent me to do all these works, for I have not done them of my own will. If these men die naturally like all men, or if they are visited by the common fate of all men, then the LORD has not sent me. But if the LORD creates a new thing, and the earth opens its mouth and swallows them up with all that belongs to them, and they go down alive into the pit, then you will understand that these men have rejected the LORD'" (Num. 16:28-30).

---

[15] Covered further in the Chapter, "Iniquity and the world"

As soon as he said those words, the ground opened up beneath them and the three men, along with their households and tents, fell into the giant rift and the earth closed over them once more.

It was not only Korah, Dathan and Abiram whose lives came to an early end at the hand of a righteous God, but their "wives, sons and young children" as well. These men sinned by seeking the glory, prestige and honor of a ministry that was not theirs to have. In essence, the same iniquity was found in them as in the Father of Lies when he, as Lucifer, sought for a glory and honor that was not his and refused to fulfill his God-given purpose.

Another famous story of God's wrath was when He destroyed the cities of Sodom and Gomorrah. The women and children perished along with the wicked men. Another element of that story was Lot's wife, who also perished when she looked back at the city when it was going up in smoke. She made the decision to look back, but Lot was the one who had chosen to live in the sinful city in the first place. He barely survived with his life and that of his two daughters—whose lives and futures were also negatively affected by their father's iniquitized decisions [Gen. 19].

You can doubtless find a number of similar stories, throughout the Bible and on down through history, of "iniquitized" decisions that affected not only the individual involved but the families and children as well. In the world today, many men have blatantly chosen not to provide for their families in any way. Too many children today are being raised without a proper foundation. They lack the influence of a healthy male figure and the effects are greater than many would imagine. The following facts, though eye-opening and depressing, are at the same time not altogether surprising:

86% of teenage suicides happen in fatherless families.

Children from broken homes are significantly more likely to suffer from mental disturbances.

> *Children of divorced parents find it significantly more difficult, when they are grown, to develop a lasting relationship with a partner.*[16]

These statistics are somewhat easy to gather. It would be virtually impossible, however, to garner statistics that outline the effects of *every* iniquitous decision on the part of the father on his wife and children. Iniquity affects people of every religion, every class in society, and every race. Right now, only God knows just how pervasively iniquity has entered humanity. One day, however, He will open His books, and what is hidden will be laid out clearly for all to see.

A recent movie titled "Courageous" shows just how pervasive iniquity is in the lives of men in the church today. Courageous[17] follows the lives of five Christian fathers as they grapple with their faith, life's challenges, and their callings as husbands and fathers.

Casting Crowns, a popular Christian band, wrote the theme song for the movie. The song is also called "Courageous." A few lines of the song state:

> *We were made to be courageous*
>
> *We were made to lead the way*
>
> *We could be the generation that finally breaks the chains*

The song makes an observation:

> *We were warriors on the front lines*
>
> *Standing unafraid*
>
> *But now we're watchers on the side lines*
>
> *While our families slip away.*

---

[16] Lowman, Pete. A Long Way East of Eden: Could God Explain the Mess We're In? Paternoster: 2002.

[17] Kendrick, Alex [Director]. Kendrick, Stephen [Producer]. Courageous [Motion picture.] Studio: Provident Films and Affirm Films. Tristar Pictures [Distributors].

And then it gives a call that needs to resound in the hearts of all Christian men today:

Where are you men of courage?

You were made for so much more.

Let the pounding of our hearts cry,

"We will serve the Lord."[18]

It takes courage to buck the tide of iniquity, to stand against lethargy, compromise, pride, and the many other outcroppings of iniquity in one's life. Yet this is the calling of every man of God today.

Beware of Judgment

Only God can judge whether or not a person is fulfilling their God-ordained purpose. From the outside, it could look like someone is leading a great Christian life, doing wonderful things and leading a fruitful ministry, yet in reality perhaps God had called that person to forsake all and be a missionary on a foreign field, bringing the Gospel of the Kingdom of God to those who have not heard it. That individual's life is failing to follow his predesigned purpose.

On the other hand, someone could be a wealthy doctor who rarely goes to church because she is on call and works on the weekend. However, she has been called to a ministry of counseling teenagers who are pregnant and considering abortion. She gives Godly and Christian counseling and refers them to places that can help them.

---

[18] Mark Hall and Matthew West. Courageous [Recorded by Casting Crowns]. On *Come to the Well*. Zoo Studio: Beach Street.

One of these ministries might seem less important and even less of a "Christian" calling, yet it is ordained by God and therefore freer of iniquity than one that might look "right" on the outside yet in reality it is not that individual's purpose and plan. It all comes down to finding God's will for one's life, which might sound very difficult, especially if one doesn't know whether it is even possible to hear His voice speaking in their hearts.

More on this topic will be covered in my next book, but in short, anyone who has sensed the voice of God's Word speaking to their hearts has the ability to hear His voice and therefore has the power to follow His plan for their life.

His Perfect Plan

Not every person—man or woman—is ordained to marry and build a family, yet each one is ordained to create and fulfill the purpose God has written for their lives. Within the limited realm of their particular situations and circumstances, every human on this earth can still make the decisions and has the power to create through their God-given ordination: "Ye have not chosen me but I have chosen you and ordained you that you should go and bring forth fruit and that your fruit should remain" (John 15:16a). We cannot choose *what* our calling and purpose will be. We can only choose whether or not we will be *faithful* to the calling that is given us.

God has promised that we will "bear fruit," but only He knows the time and the way in which our efforts will finally be fruitful. All that we are called to do is follow His plan, even if things do not turn out as we might hope or plan. The picture that we see is "through a glass darkly." Only when we are "face to face" (1 Cor. 13:12a) with Him will we see all that has gone on behind the scenes and realize that it was a part of His plan.

Although many have been negatively affected by the iniquity of their parents in some form or another, there is still hope.

Every born-again believer has the power to be completely healed and restored of the effects of iniquity. They can go on to pursue a successful and productive life according to their preordained destiny. "If anyone is in Christ, he is a new creation; old things have passed away; behold, all things have become new" (2 Cor. 5:17).

⌘

CHAPTER SUMMARY:

- Iniquity has brought about far-reaching negative effects on the family structure, creating an overall breakdown to the family unit.

- A man can provide for his family in a variety of ways: with food, shelter, finances, clothing, protection, education, vacations and many other basic needs and wants. However, if he fails to provide for them *spiritually*, he has failed to provide the most important foundation that his family needs.

- Too many children today are being raised without a proper foundation. They lack the influence of a healthy male figure and the effects are more devastating than many would imagine.

- We cannot choose what our calling and purpose will be. We can only choose whether or not we will be faithful to the calling that is given us.

- Anyone who has sensed the voice of God's Word speaking to their hearts has the ability to hear His voice and therefore has the power to follow His plan for their life.

- Although many have been negatively affected by iniquity, every born-again believer has the power to be completely healed and restored of the effects of iniquity, going on to pursue a productive life according to their preordained destiny.

APPLICATION:

1. Write down ways in which you feel iniquity has affected your personal family unit. If there are things that you currently do not have the power to change, commit them to God in prayer and trust that He can and will work everything for your good and that of your family. If there are things you can work on changing and improving, pray about them and create a step-by-step plan to do so.

2. If you were raised without a parent or feel that those that raised you did not nurture or equip you properly for life, consider pursuing mentors for your future. If you are a male, search for spiritually mature male figures that can nurture and strengthen your manhood in any area that you feel you need strengthening and development. If you are a female, search for spiritually mature female figures that can nurture and strengthen your womanhood in any areas that you feel that you need strengthening and development.

CHAPTER 10
INIQUITY AND THE WORLD

"Let's pray that the human race never escapes from the Earth to spread its iniquity elsewhere." – C.S. Lewis

There is so much uncertainty and confusion in the world today. One has only to turn on their television or look at the headlines of their newspaper to see the downward spiral as the world itself seems to be heading straight for destruction.

The Root Reason

Terrorism is a daily concern and topic. Many countries have no solutions to combat the spread of deadly diseases; starvation affects their people. Many governments are composed of different political groups that constantly demonstrate division on a variety of topics, and fail to follow through with promises that they have made to better the plights of the people. In these governments, there are those who have been found guilty of political corruption and even moral failures. Leaders of nations are willing to compromise their religious beliefs and consent to a form of moral relativity, ignoring the absolutes that have been in place for thousands of years.

Today, the main message being preached through the media is "do what feels right for you," regardless of whether it truly is right or wrong, and how it affects others. This attitude has become so prevalent that many believe there are no absolutes of right and wrong. Instead, morals are "relative," based on the individual's system of values and beliefs.

If you haven't guessed it yet, iniquity is the root cause of all the problems that the world faces today.

"God is not the author of confusion" (1 Cor. 14:33). Looking around us at the issues that plague the world, they are confusing and complex. Clearly, God has not authored the "story" that is unfolding across the world today. God is the author of peace, truth, love and justice [1 Cor. 14:33, Ex. 34:6, 1 John 4:8, Deut. 10:18].

Iniquity has caused so many in the world today to follow after an unseen god of this world, Satan, and play parts in his "master plan" rather than in God's perfect plan. Satan's biggest trick is to convince the world that he doesn't exist. Is there hope, then, for this world before it meets with a sad and terrible end?

The Olive Mountain Prophecy

The truth is that many of these issues and problems were foretold thousands of years ago as signs to watch for. Jesus' vision traversed thousands of years and gave us the ability to know what is to come beyond the evil times that we face today.

> "Now as He sat on the Mount of Olives, the disciples came to Him privately, saying, 'Tell us, when will these things be? And what will be the sign of Your coming, and of the end of the age?'" (Matt. 24:3)

He began to speak, giving them a list of signs to look out for that would show the end of the age was approaching.

> "And Jesus answered and said to them: 'Take heed that no one deceives you. For many will come in My name, saying, "I am the Christ," and will deceive many'" (Matt. 24:4-5).

If you wanted to check the authenticity of this statement, you have to look no further than your computer. Google "I am Christ" and you'll find a number of people who have claimed to be Christ in recent times. Many of these, in their sad delusion, have hurt people or intended to do so, and have deceived others. We know by the verse that there will be more to come.

This deception could also include people who function in the ministries of what is traditionally called the fivefold ministry—Pastors, Teachers, Evangelists, Apostles and Prophets [Eph. 4:11-14].

I have personally been taught and influenced by people who function in one or another of these five ministries. I have served in a couple of these roles myself. I now realize that I was deceiving people due to the fact that I was unknowingly infected with iniquity. Though I was not deceiving people deliberately, I failed to teach the people what they needed to know because I was not being instructed by God on what to teach. I was teaching them what I had learned from others and what I thought they should know. Only on rare occasions did I give them something that literally came from God. Since making an effort to root iniquity out of my life, I have had to unlearn some things that were rooted in the manmade philosophies, traditions, and religion to which I have been exposed [Col. 2:8].

For the most part, those involved in teaching inaccurate philosophies are only imitating what they themselves have been taught. There is a huge difference between someone who teaches principles based on the true Kingdom of God, which is what Jesus taught, and someone who teaches from a perspective of denominational, philosophical or traditional "learned" religion.

These five ministries were originally intended to be gifts from God to the body of Christ to help mature the believer to a perfect (whole and complete) person that functions in the fullness and stature of Christ [Eph. 4:11-32]. If a person functioning in any of these roles is being affected by iniquity, wouldn't it be safe to assume that what they are teaching may be inaccurate or not originating in truth?

> *"And you will hear of wars and rumors of wars. See that you are not troubled, for all these things must occur; but the end is not yet"* (Matt. 24:6).

A little over a hundred years ago, inhabitants of the world hoped that "The Great War" (World War One) would be the war to end all wars.

It wasn't.

In fact, the 20th century was marked as the "bloodiest" century to date, with more victims that died in wars during that hundred-year period than died in all the wars of all the previous centuries combined.

> *"For nation will rise against nation, and kingdom against kingdom"* (Matt. 24:7a).

A more accurate translation for the word "nation" in the verse above might have been "ethnic group," stemmed from the Greek word *ethnos*. Have ethnic groups been "rising against" each other? Sadly, yes. Think for a moment of the "killing fields"—the genocide of the Khmer Rouge; the "ethnic cleansing" of the Bosnian Croats by the Bosnian Serbs; the forced relocation and ethnic cleansing of the Palestinians to where the few remaining have no place to call home; or the widely known Holocaust where horrors were committed against those of the Jewish faith. These are only a few examples of "ethnos" rising against "ethnos."

> *"And there will be famines . . ."* (Matt. 24:7b).

When we think of famine, a picture that most likely comes to mind is African children—skinny arms and bloated stomachs—reaching for help. Hundreds of millions suffer from chronic hunger and millions of children die of malnutrition every year. The horrible reality is that while millions of people are starving in developing countries, wealthy countries destroy millions of tons of food to avoid "flooding the market" and causing a drop in prices. "World hunger is rooted in a breakdown of humanitarian values," states a report by the Bread for the World Institute.[19]

"...and pestilences . . ." (Matt. 24:7b).

The advent of inoculation and many other medical breakthroughs brought a general perception that we had said goodbye to infectious diseases, that we had locked up viral and bacterial killers and thrown away the key.

How We Die, a "runaway bestseller" by Dr. Sherwin Nuland, has the following observation, which makes it clear that things are not as hopeful as we might have thought: "Medicine's claim to have triumphed over infectious disease has become an illusion."

The resurgence in diseases has its foundation in a variety of things, such as the misuse and overuse of antibiotics on humans and animals, the outbreaks of fairly new diseases like AIDS, Ebola and SARS, and the effects of years of abusing the environment.

"... and earthquakes in different places" (Matt. 24:7b).

During the 800-year period from 1000 to 1800, only 21 major earthquakes were reported. Over the next hundred years, there were 18. During the past century (1900-2000), there have been 150! The new century, since 2000, has marked an explosion in number of earthquakes. Over a hundred major earthquakes have occurred each year, and nearly every year, there has been at least one earthquake with a magnitude of over 8.0.[20]

"All these are the beginning of sorrows" (Matt. 24:8).

---

[19] "800 Million Go Hungry in Developing Nations." Associated Press. 14 Oct. 1994.
[20] "Earthquake Facts and Statistics." Earthquake.usgs.gov. *U.S. Geological Survey – U.S. Department of the Interior.* 25 Apr. 2012. Accessed 4 May 2012.

These many horrors have brought sorrow throughout the world, and there will be more to come.

Why is all of this happening?

*"Because **iniquity** shall abound, the love of many will become cold"* (Matt. 24:12).

Most of these issues—wars, famines, even plagues and diseases—can be attributed to love growing "cold" in the hearts of people worldwide. Selfishness, greed, hate and pride are all borne of iniquity.

Iniquity is the underlying cause of these problems in the world today, from famine to wars, from sorrow to persecution, from disease to pestilences. Iniquity—the lack of knowledge of the truth being applied in the decisions one makes in his or her life, resulting in a life lived in ways other than it is meant to be.

The earth itself and every person that lives in it is affected by iniquity, some in greater ways than others, yet through the redeeming power of Christ and the guidance of His Holy Spirit, there is no one whose life cannot be completely turned around and transformed to be free from iniquity and its devastating effects.

Signs of Iniquity Today

In addition to the signs mentioned in the Bible, there are many other signs and manifestations of iniquity throughout the world. Issues such as corporate greed, government oppression and the raping of the earth's resources for selfish gain are rooted in iniquity. Racial prejudice and division in religions and beliefs are rooted in pride.

Widespread problems—from lack of loving and consistent discipline to abuse of every kind, from violence in schools and communities to violence on television and in the media, from unnatural ideas and wrongful concepts being portrayed as acceptable to a spurge in depression and suicides—are all rooted in iniquity ... the love of many growing cold.

We see these effects in "micro" form in millions of families, and in the lives of individuals, across country lines and generations. Zoom out a bit and we can see larger images of iniquity portrayed by governments and nations. Zoom out further and it is apparent throughout the entire world.

It's a picture of lives that have succumbed to selfishness, greed and pride—iniquity—rather than choosing a defined and positive purpose.

Yet Jesus promises hope.

"But he who endures to the end, the same shall be kept safe" (Matt. 24:13).

Enduring does not mean just hiding away, hoping that things will get better. Synonyms of endurance are "persistence," "continuousness," and "durability." Endurance is remaining strong, continuing to persist on the path to which one has been called by God. "The same shall be kept safe."

We will not only be kept safe, but called to stand up and be counted as one of Christ's own through preaching the Gospel, incidentally the next "sign."

City on a Hill

"And this gospel of the kingdom shall be proclaimed in all the world as a witness to all nations" (Matt. 24:14).

Try to guess the most watched film of all time. Titanic? Lord of the Rings? Twilight? Guess again.

The Jesus Film ... has been watched by more than two billion people. ...

At first sight, Jesus, or the Jesus Film as it has come to be known, is an unlikely candidate for the title of most watched – and most translated – film. Shot on location in the Holy Land, and with a white British Jesus, it is instead a straight-faced retelling of Luke's gospel. It was made in 1979 ...

But how, while it is virtually unknown in the UK and many other Western countries, did it ever receive such an enormous worldwide audience? And how did it get translated into more than 760 languages and dialects, among them Uyghur, Jorai, Karakalpak, Hakka, Mongo-Nkudu and Nosu Yi?

The reason is simply the work of an American evangelical organization, Campus Crusade. Funded by its supporters and well-wishers, it sends teams around the world, even where they are not particularly welcome. There they record new translations of the film, organize screenings to inquisitive crowds in improvised cinemas, and distribute copies to whoever they can.

The Campus Crusade is only one organization focused on doing a great work. There are many more. With today's modern means of communication—Facebook, email, e-books, Twitter, and more—the opportunities for spreading the Gospel of the Kingdom of God are unprecedented.

The Gospel of the Kingdom is going to be preached in all the world, and not a moment too soon.

Think of certain people of whom it is clear, by looking at their lives and missions, that they have fulfilled their purpose in life. It is wonderful and amazing to realize how much can be accomplished by one person, when they are faithful to follow the path that God has charted for them.

It is also sad to realize that those kinds of people can be counted on one hand. There are so few of them in the world today, which is why they stand as shining lights.

We are told that we who believe in Jesus are meant to be like a city set on a hill, one that cannot be hidden [Matt. 5:14]. If more believers would choose to shine as lights in the darkness, the world would begin to glow with the light of a thousand, and then a million, separate flames. Some would combine to become blazes and start to set other fires until the whole world could be ablaze with the light and truth of God's love, direction and purpose.

The problems throughout the world might seem too big, too vast, too great, too complicated and complex for you to make a difference. You do not have to change the entire world in one shot. You can't. Yet you can change your own little part, starting with yourself and your own life, and moving on outward to greater things until you will find that the world is beginning to change. Perhaps your purpose is only changing a small part of your world, but who knows? Perhaps you will be called to do greater things than you ever imagined.

In any case, you are called according to His purpose and if you follow that call, the effects will be greater than you can imagine and your reward will be great, now and for eternity.

⌘

Chapter Summary:

- Iniquity is the root cause of most, if not all, of the problems across the world today.

- Iniquity has caused so many in the world today to follow after an unseen god of this world, Satan, and play parts in his "master plan" rather than in God's perfect plan.

- There is a huge difference between someone who teaches principles based on the true Kingdom of God, which is what Jesus taught, and someone who teaches from a perspective of denominational, philosophical or traditional "learned" religion.

- Many of these issues we face, brought on by iniquity, were foretold by Jesus Christ thousands of years ago.

- We might not be able to change the whole world, but we can do that which we have been called and ordained to do, and by doing so, begin to change the world for the better.

Application:

1. Do you find that you are discouraged, fearful or hopeless about what is happening in the world today? Consider what your perception has been up to this point. Seek God as to what your reaction should be to any issues that affect you, and even those that might not directly affect you.

2. Ask God how you can be "a shining light in the midst of darkness." Ask Him to reveal your purpose and how you can be an answer to a problem in the world.

CHAPTER 11

JESUS AND INIQUITY

"I will say to them, 'I never knew you, depart from me, you that practice iniquity." – Jesus

The Spotless Lamb

Before I understood the root meaning of "iniquity," the words of Jesus in Matthew 7:21-23 puzzled and even frightened me. I wondered why He would respond the way He did to people who were doing good things in His name:

> *"Not everyone that saith unto me, Lord, Lord, shall enter into the kingdom of heaven; but he that doeth the will of my Father which is in heaven. Many will say to me in that day, Lord, Lord, have we not prophesied in thy name? And in thy name have cast out devils? And in thy name done many wonderful works? And then will I profess unto them, I never knew you: depart from me, ye that work iniquity"* (Matt. 7:21-23, KJV)[21].

These people were doing great things, prophesying in the name of the Lord, casting out devils and performing wondrous works. All of these seem to be great deeds that should have pleased God. Jesus clearly stated why all of this was not good enough. The fact that

---

[21] In this chapter, I'm using King James Version of the Bible, which uses the word "iniquity" from the translation of the original manuscripts. Other translations have substituted this key word with words such as wicked, evil, and lawlessness—which are results or manifestations of iniquity.

they "work iniquity" cancels not only their good deeds but also their placement in the Kingdom of Heaven.

The words "I never knew you" are words that we never want to hear coming out of the mouth of God.

Of course, God knows or has an awareness of us because He created every human being. The word "knew" in this passage is a reference to when one is intimate with another. For example, in the Old Testament when a man "knew" his wife this meant that they had sexual intercourse, which often resulted in conception.

God desires to have a relational intercourse with every human so that the seed of His truth will impregnate us with the revelation of the pure knowledge of who we are in Christ and who He really is. He wants us to conceive and produce His will through our lives on this earth. When we allow God to pour the power of His truth into our minds, when we use it to create the works that have been predestined for us to do, only then are we functioning in the perfect will of God [Rom. 8:28, Eph. 1:11 & 2:10]. The presence of iniquity perverts and cancels this process.

God is a God of truth and there is no iniquity in Him [Deut. 32:4]. For the salvation of humanity, God required a spotless lamb, a sacrifice that was free of iniquity. The seed of God provided through the Holy Spirit was the only seed absent of the impurities of iniquity. In essence, God provided His own seed, which produced His very own Son [2 Cor. 5:19].

The Straight and Narrow Way

In the following key passages, Jesus was asked a very important question: "Are there few that be saved?" Jesus clearly states that strait, or narrow, is the gate or entryway that one must take to be saved. He also addresses an important fact that many just read and pass over because they assume that they are in right standing with God:

> "Then said one unto him, 'Lord, are there few that be saved?' And he said unto them, 'Strive to enter in at the strait gate: for many, I say unto you, will seek to enter in, and shall not be able. When once the master of the house is risen up, and hath shut to the door, and ye begin to stand without, and to knock at the door, saying, Lord, Lord, open unto us; and he shall answer and say unto you, I know you not whence ye are: Then shall ye begin to say, We have eaten and drunk in thy presence, and thou hast taught in our streets. But he shall say, I tell you, I know you not whence ye are; depart from me, **all ye workers of iniquity**. There shall be weeping and gnashing of teeth, when ye shall see Abraham, and Isaac, and Jacob, and all the prophets, in the kingdom of God, and you yourselves thrust out'" (Luke 13:22-28, KJV).

These people assumed they were saved since they had fellowshipped with Jesus in their eating and drinking; they were even taught by Him. This is a picture of many deceived believers today: they believe they have fellowship with Him in drinking the spiritual milk and eating the meat of the Word of God through the traditional teaching that they believe comes from God. Yet, once again, iniquity blinds people to the reality of their true condition and standing before God. Jesus mentions this same "strait" gate in the following passages:

> "Enter ye in at the strait gate: for wide is the gate, and broad is the way, that leadeth to destruction, and many there be which go in thereat: Because strait is the gate, and narrow is the way, which leadeth unto life, and few there be that find it" (Matt. 7:13-14, KJV).

It is impossible to enter into this strait and narrow gate with the weight of iniquity. It is very important to note Jesus' specific words. He states that "few find" the "strait and narrow gate." Those that have positioned themselves to embrace the truth of God's purpose for their lives and cast away iniquity are those who will find the strait and narrow way.

Grace and Truth Revisited

You might find within these words a challenge to traditional thinking, knowledge and teaching, yet the gospel of grace has been reduced in many religious environments to a doctrine that accommodates grace as a remedy for sin instead of a portal for truth that introduces answers to remove the grip of sin and its root cause: iniquity. Though the Bible is very clear in that God is a forgiving God if we confess our sins, God's provision of grace is not a license to sin. It is not a reason for one to avoid dealing with their sinful nature and behavior, of which iniquity is the root cause.

The Greek word for grace is charis, which is traditionally defined as "unmerited favor." The Hebrew word for grace is *chên*. The *Ancient Hebrew Lexicon of the Bible* defines this word as "beauty." This form of beauty is defined through three key illustrations that describe a camp setting. The first illustration comes in the form of an instruction: "to erect a tent." The second illustration describes this camp setting as "a place of freedom that is protected." The third illustration is a Hebrew metaphor that describes grace as "streams of water."[22]

When combined, these three illustrations reveal God's original purpose for grace. The original understanding of grace is derived from the Bible's first mention of grace, found in Genesis Chapter six, verse eight: "But Noah found grace in the eyes of the Lord" (Gen. 6:8). Noah was given *detailed instructions* from God to build an ark [Gen. 6:11-22]. The ark itself represented the *tent* or a housing that would provide *protection* for him and his family from the *streams of water* known as *the flood* that God would send to cleanse the earth of evil [Gen. 6:5-7].

The book of Numbers Chapter 2 also illustrates the grace of God. In this chapter, *detailed instructions* were also given by God through Moses for the Israelites to pitch their *tents* around the tabernacle according to their individual tribes. God displayed

---

[22] See appendix for resources used to research the original understanding of grace.

His favor and *protection* toward them in that He provided *order* for the Israelites when they moved from place to place. The Israelites would always assemble the tabernacle and their *tents* near a water source, hence the "streams of water." What must be captured by these two examples are that if Noah or the Israelites would have deviated or completely neglected the instructions from God, the *protection* of His grace would not have been available.

These illustrations or definitions don't make too much sense when we put them up against the definition of grace used in traditional religious settings, which is "unmerited favor." However, when you combine these three original Hebrew concepts for grace of *tents*, *protection* and *water*, the passages found in John Chapter 1, verses 14 and 17 make clear sense. These passages state that Jesus came to the earth "full of grace and truth." In other words, God provided grace through *protection* through Jesus, who was sent as a *tent* or a housing that *produced freedom* through the *order of detailed instructions* that came out of His mouth, *streams of water*—which is a descriptive metaphor for The Word of God.

This also makes clearer another profound statement that Jesus made when He said, "He who believes on Me, as the Scripture has said, 'Out of his belly shall flow rivers of living water'" (John 7:38). This verse gives us the illustration of a believer who positions themselves as a *tent* (a temple of God) where living words (truth) are dispersed from their inner being, which produces *freedom* that is designed by God to *protect* that individual. A spirit-filled believer is endowed with the same access of life-sustaining qualities that Jesus came to earth with, which are a full capacity of grace and truth, yet these must be properly understood and applied.

The famous song "Amazing Grace" was penned by John Newton, an English clergyman and writer, after he converted to Christianity and abandoned his participation in the slave trade. In his song, he said "how sweet the sound," not "how sweet the thing," which is what many religions have reduced grace to. Grace is meant to be a housing that disperses the sound of truth through streams of living water designed to deliver a sound that nurtures and cleanses all that need it—which is every human being that has ever existed.

Grace and truth can never be separated [Col. 1:6]. Jesus introduced God's favor towards mankind through His gifts of grace and truth [John 1:14, 17]. The *beauty* of the grace of God is literally that there is a "truth remedy" to whatever is wrong with you. The only one that can legally prescribe this remedy is the great Physician (God) Himself. This prescription will always come in a dose of detailed information (truth), yet unless one accepts it through a spiritual "gestation," wholeness and restoration will never take place. The purpose and function of grace is misunderstood in the hearts of many believers today. Grace has become just as ineffective as a placebo given to someone, leaving the false impression that something positive took place. True grace should always produce truth that cleanses, nurtures, protects and transforms.

Hebrews 10:26 states, "For if we sin willfully after we have received the knowledge of the truth, there remains no more sacrifice for sins." One of the main reasons many continue to sin willfully is because grace has been taught in such a way that it reduces the responsibility of man. The assumption is that because we have been forgiven for our sins, it is no longer necessary to remedy sinful behavior. Many today have not received the knowledge of truth at the level that is needed for them to effectively deal with sin in their lives. Until this is remedied, it will keep a believer from accurately understanding who he/she is in Christ and what his/her purpose in life is.

> *If we say that we have fellowship with Him and walk in darkness, we lie and* **do not practice the truth**. *But if we walk in the light, as He is in the light, we have fellowship with one another, and the blood of Jesus Christ His Son cleanses us from all sin. If we say that we have no sin, we deceive ourselves, and the truth is not in us. If we confess our sins, He is faithful and just to forgive us our sins,* **and to cleanse us from all unrighteousness**. *If we say that we have not sinned, we make Him a liar, and* **His Word is not in us** (1 John 1:6-10).

Paul encouraged the believers at Corinth to do a self examination. This applies to every believer today. This self examination should be a consistent daily practice in a Christian's life.

> *"Examine yourselves, whether you are in the faith, prove your own selves. Do you not know your own selves, that Jesus Christ is in you, unless you are reprobates?" (2 Cor. 13:5)*

The question carries a responsibility to understand that the same spiritual presence and power that was in Jesus abides in every spirit-filled believer. The word reprobate means "one that is unapproved, rejected, castaway, and worthless." The absence of truth awareness and application cancels the powerful impact of the presence and power of God in one's life. It reduces the believer's experience to a traditionalized, impotent religious existence instead of one that is an all-powerful representation of the Kingdom of Heaven.

King David, who is known as a man after God's own heart, asked for help in the area of self examination:

> *"Search me, O God, and know my heart: try me, and know my thoughts: And see if there be any wicked way in me, and lead me in the way everlasting" (Ps. 139:23-24).*

This vital request to have God search the heart has become one of my regular requests in prayer. I ask God for His help in making me aware of any area in my life where iniquity is manifested. It's like taking an inventory of the heart to make sure that nothing is present that would reduce the truth of who I am and who God requires me to be.

Spirit and Truth

When Jesus had a key conversation with a Samaritan woman in John Chapter 4, He shared with her one of most profound statements that is found in the Bible; this passage has been misunderstood by many. Let's take a deeper look at Jesus' conversation with the Samaritan woman:

> *"Jesus saith unto her, Woman, believe me, the hour cometh, when ye shall neither in this mountain, nor yet at Jerusalem, worship the Father. Ye worship ye know not what: we know what we worship: for salvation is of the Jews. But the hour cometh, and now is, when the true worshippers shall worship the Father in spirit and in truth: for the Father seeketh such to worship Him. God is a Spirit: and they that worship Him must worship Him in spirit and in truth"* (John 4:22-24, KJV).

The key ingredients to the worship that Jesus mentioned were "spirit" and "truth." Let's define them to gain a better understanding of what God required in our worship. In both mentions of "spirit," the "s" is not capitalized, whereas in the phrase "God is a Spirit," it is capitalized. However, both words have the same meaning.

In Greek, the word "spirit" is *pneuma*, which means "a current of air that is breathed." In the original Hebrew, the word is *ruach*, meaning "the wind of God or man, enlargement, inspiration, breath of life."

The word "truth" in Greek is *aletheia*, which simply means "verity or reality." In Hebrew, the word is *emet*, which means "what is established, right, sure, faithful, firm, original information or meaning, what nurtures the covenant."

While on earth, Jesus only spoke and did what He received from God the Father. Jesus defined this as "truth" [John 5:19, 30, 36; 8:40, 45; 16:7; 17:17]. He also called the Holy Spirit the "Spirit of Truth" [John 14:17, 15:26, 16:13].

The ultimate goal of every believer should be to learn to hear, see, speak and do just like Jesus did. In order to live life accurately, we must capture this pure process of interaction with God. We can see throughout the Gospels that Jesus was the original true worshipper; He was inspired constantly with original information, truth that nurtured the agreement that He had with God the Father.

This truth contained the detailed instructions and will of God for His life. Jesus inhaled or took this truth into His spirit and then exhaled back to God through His words and actions of complete obedience. The purest form of worship is honoring and reverencing God by exhaling back to Him—through complete obedience—the instructions that are deposited into us. In so doing, we nurture the covenant that He has with us. This is worship "in spirit and truth" at the highest level.

God breathes the instruction-filled power of truth into you through the virtue of His Spirit. The loins of your mind (or your heart) are supposed to creatively reproduce all that you hear and see from God the Father. This is what Jesus did; we, as spirit-filled believers, have the potential to do the same. Iniquity hinders and perverts this process, rendering it impotent.

Without the purity of truth, we will never know God for who and what He is. Truth is the purest form of knowledge. Truth is the language of Heaven. Without the purity of truth, we will also never know who we really are. God is the only one authorized to tell you the truth or original information about who you are.

I often ask people the question, "Do you believe that there is more to you and life than what you are experiencing?" The answer has always been, "Yes." The Spirit of Truth is the only one authorized to show us that "more to us and life" that all too often continues to escape us because of the absence of truth.

This vital information can only come through the combination of His written Word—the Bible—and the voice of His spoken word. God will always speak through the Spirit of Truth, which is pure and free of iniquity. It is imperative for every believer to hear the voice of God for themselves.

Gospel of the Kingdom

> *"If you have not chosen The Kingdom of God first, it will in the end make no difference what you have chosen instead." – William Law*

Jesus was and still is what I call a Kingdom Man [John 18:36]. Even though Jesus was born as a human on this earth, He understood that the Holy Spirit resided within Him and that His original being was not earthly, but Heavenly. This is a concept that many Christians today fail to completely understand, especially since this same concept of spiritual origin also applies to every human.

At the start of His earthly ministry, Jesus introduced and taught the Gospel of the Kingdom of God and of Heaven [Matt. 4:17, 23, 6:33, 9:35, 24:14]. Throughout the first four books of the New Testament that record Jesus' earthly life and ministry, Jesus constantly referred to "the Kingdom."

The word Gospel means "good news" or "good message." Jesus' good news came straight from Heaven. It did not come from an earthly source [John 8:28, 38, 12:49]. Every Apostle, Prophet, Pastor, Evangelist and Teacher on the earth today should also be a Kingdom man or woman and teach the Gospel of the Kingdom of God.

I have taken a number of religious courses and have spoken to many people who have graduated from well-known Bible colleges. People who attend Bible colleges are taught how to prepare a sermon, how to perform a ministry, how to memorize the 66 books of the Bible, and how to use different studying techniques. They study the philosophy of the founders of many different religions today. But when I asked those that I know who have graduated from Bible colleges how many courses they had on gaining a root understanding of the Kingdom of God, the answer was always, "None." It would be safe to assume that if these same people were asked how many classes were they taught on the root understanding of iniquity, the answer more than likely would be the same: "None." There are thousands of Christians receiving religious training yet not one class is offered on the main topic that Jesus taught—the Kingdom of God—or on iniquity, of which the devil was originally guilty and continues to use against humanity.

Though it is, of course, important to receive spiritual training from earthly organizations, it is vital that these organizations are teaching that which comes from a true Kingdom foundation—information and training that lines up with the teachings of Jesus. Unfortunately, many today are getting their messages and training from earthly sources and not from God Himself.

The Gospel of the Kingdom of God is only, and will always only be, truth based. This Gospel is without any trace of iniquity; it originates from Heaven. In order to return to the original message and purpose of God—the pure Gospel, iniquity has to be removed. The reality is that iniquity has been allowed to contaminate the Gospel of the Kingdom.

Iniquity keeps one from having a true, Kingdom-of-Heaven mindset. Though someone may get their information and training from an earthly source—such as a Bible college, home Bible study or discipleship course—if it doesn't come from a true Kingdom-of-Heaven perspective, chances are strong that some type of iniquitized knowledge is present.

It is impossible to be accurately and consistently led by the Spirit of God unless iniquity is first rooted out. In other words, a son of God has to be free of iniquity, such as our God-given model, Jesus.

Within many churches today, ministers are mishandling the Word of God. They have a form of godliness on the outside and through their words but are guilty of handling the sacred Word of God deceitfully. This is usually not a conscious action, but is due to the hold of iniquity upon their lives and ministry. Though I know that these are strong words, an honest assessment is needed to reveal the sad fact that the truth of God has been rendered vain and powerless in many churches today. God's truth is being used for purposes other than what God originally intended.

> *"Therefore seeing we have this ministry, as we have received mercy, we faint not; But have renounced the hidden things of dishonesty, not walking in craftiness, nor handling the word of God deceitfully;* **but by manifestation of the truth** *commending ourselves to every man's conscience in the sight of God. But if our gospel be hid, it is hid to them that are lost: In whom the god of this world hath blinded the minds of them which believe not, lest the light of the glorious gospel of Christ, who is the image of God, should shine unto them"* (2 Cor. 4:1-4).

Jesus dealt with this same perverted condition when He confronted the religious ministers of His day. Jesus warned the people of the "iniquitized" condition through the imagery of the baking ingredient of leaven. It takes only a small amount to affect the whole loaf of bread. Likewise, all it takes is a little bit of iniquity to affect the entire body of believers [See 1 Cor. 5:6-7, Gal. 5:9].

> *"Then Jesus said unto them, Take heed and beware of the leaven of the Pharisees and of the Sadducees"* (Matt. 16:6).

> *"Then they understood that He did not say to beware of the leaven of bread, but of* **the doctrine** *of the Pharisees and Sadducees"* (Matt. 16:12).

Jesus was constantly exposing the religious leaders of His day. One would think that those that taught and supposedly practiced the law of God should have gotten it right. These men were leaders and teachers in the synagogues of that day; many of them would have gone to rabbinical school starting as early as the age of six, not completing their studies until the age of about 30, which is when the title of rabbi was given. This would be similar to our churches today, in that many ministers spend years in Sunday school and other church-offered ministries before going on to seminary school and then Bible College.

> *"Woe to you, scribes and Pharisees, hypocrites! For you pay tithes of mint and dill and cummin, and you have left undone the weightier matters of the Law, judgment, mercy, and faith. You*

> ought to have done these and not to leave the other undone. Blind guides who strain out a gnat and swallow a camel! Woe to you, scribes and Pharisees, hypocrites! For you cleanse the outside of the cup and of the dish, but inside they are full of extortion and excess. Blind Pharisee! First cleanse the inside of the cup and of the dish, so that the outside of them may be clean also. Woe to you, scribes and Pharisees, hypocrites! For you are like whitewashed tombs, which indeed appear beautiful outside, but inside they are full of dead men's bones, and of all uncleanness. Even so you also appear righteous to men outwardly, but inside you are full of hypocrisy and iniquity" (Matt. 23:23-28).

Here we see Jesus addressing these leaders and telling them that they were doing good things, yet the presence of iniquity in their lives caused them to be hypocrites. They dressed and acted the part but their insides were like dead men's bones with no life; they were blind to the purity of who God is and what His law meant. They were misleading those they taught and putting requirements on the people that God never instructed them to do. The presence of iniquity can cause extortion and false, manmade expressions of righteousness.

Jesus attributed their ways of error to hypocrisy that was rooted in iniquity. If Jesus brought correction in that day to those who spent years in training to minister the law of God, then the Holy Spirit can bring correction to us today, highlighting any erroneous ways that are rooted in iniquity. The purpose for this correction would be so that we can accurately minister the law and truth of God through the Gospel of the Kingdom of God and Heaven.

In the parable of the wheat and tares [Matt. 13:24-30], Jesus once again makes it clear that the Word of God can become contaminated through the deception of the devil—the original worker of iniquity.

> "Then Jesus sent the multitude away, and went into the house: and his disciples came unto him, saying, 'Declare unto us the parable of the tares of the field.' He answered and said unto them, 'He that soweth the good seed is the Son of man; the field is the world; the

good seed are the children of the kingdom; but the tares are the children of the wicked one; the enemy that sowed them is the devil; the harvest is the end of the world; and the reapers are the angels. As therefore the tares are gathered and burned in the fire; so shall it be in the end of this world. The Son of man shall send forth his angels, and they shall gather out of his kingdom all things that offend, and them which do iniquity" (Matt. 13:37-41, KJV).

Wheat and tares look the same when viewing them with the natural eye; you cannot tell the difference. The same can be true of believers, even in a traditional church setting. From a distance—and maybe even close up—we look alike, yet the "tares" are those that have a form of Godliness but deny its true power through allowing negative influences to be implanted in their heart. If the tare is allowed to stay, it will begin to manifest all kinds of negative behaviors [See 2 Tim. 3:1-8]. One can be in a healthy environment, yet be "ever learning, and never able to come to the knowledge of the truth." Iniquity causes the inner man of one's life to be deaf and blind to pure truth, causing disorder that in many cases is accepted and soon becomes "the norm."

One of the saddest effects of iniquity in the church today is the perversion of the Gospel that Jesus taught. I had mentioned before that one of the primary principles of the Bible is the principle of the seed. The most important parable that Jesus taught on that topic was the parable of the soils [See Matt. 13:1-23, Mark 4:1-20, Luke 8:4-15]. The reason I say it was the most important is because of what Jesus Himself said in Mark 4:13: "And He said to them, do you not know this parable? And how then will you know all parables?"

The seed in this parable was the word of the Kingdom of God. This is pure seed (word) that comes from Heaven. If the pure seed of the Kingdom of God (His word or message) were taught and preached, there wouldn't be the division of beliefs and impotence of power that is currently present in these institutions. The law of the seed is this: a seed will always reproduce what is inside of it. The seed of the word (the message of the Kingdom) will always reproduce itself. Unfortunately, much of what is being taught in many religious institutions today—including churches, Bible colleges, synagogues and other spiritual environments—has been infiltrated with counterfeit seed that many claim to be of the Kingdom. However, the fruit of what is being produced is no way like the Kingdom of God. Allow me once again to encourage you to read Dr. Myles Munroe's book, *Rediscovering the Kingdom*, in order to gain more insight into this current reality.

> "Beware lest anyone rob you through philosophy and vain deceit, according to the tradition of men, according to the elements of the world, and not according to Christ" (Col. 2:8).

⌘

Chapter Summary:

- The "work of iniquity" has the potential to cancel out all good deeds that are not according to the will of God in the Kingdom of Heaven.

- The words "I never knew you" are words that we never want to hear coming out of the mouth of God.

- God desires to have a relational intercourse with every human so that the seed of His truth will impregnate us with the revelation of the pure knowledge of who we are in Christ and who He really is.

- Those that have positioned themselves to embrace the truth of God's purpose for their lives and cast away iniquity are those who will find the strait and narrow way.

- The gospel of grace has been reduced in many religious environments to a doctrine that accommodates grace as a remedy for sin instead of a portal for truth that introduces an answer to remove the grip of sin and its root cause: iniquity.

- Grace and truth can never be separated. The beauty of the grace of God is that there is a "truth remedy" to whatever is wrong with you. True grace should always produce truth that cleanses, nurtures, protects and transforms.

- The absence of truth awareness and application cancels out the powerful impact of the presence and power of God in one's life. It reduces the believer's experience to a traditionalized, impotent religious existence instead of one that is an all-powerful representation of the Kingdom of Heaven.

- This ultimate goal of every believer should be to learn to hear, see, speak and do just like Jesus did.

- The purest form of worship is honoring and reverencing God by exhaling back to Him—through complete obedience—the instructions that are deposited into us. In so doing, we nurture the covenant that He has with us. This is worship "in spirit and truth" at the highest level.

- The Gospel of the Kingdom of God is only, and will always only be, truth based. This Gospel is without any trace of iniquity; it originates from Heaven. In order to return to the original message and purpose of God—the pure Gospel—iniquity has to be removed.

Application:

1. Reflect on your newfound knowledge of the significance of the interconnection of grace and truth. Begin to make the necessary adjustments to your belief system to incorporate this original perspective of grace and truth.

2. Jesus was asked a very important question: "Are there few that be saved?" Jesus clearly states that strait and narrow is the gate or entryway that one must take to be saved. Since it is impossible to enter into this strait and narrow gate with the weight of iniquity, if you find that you need to allow the Spirit of Truth leeway to work in your life to rid it of iniquity, begin now by asking God's Spirit to work fully in your life.

3. Jesus is our example of perfection—a person of integrity; truth, whole, spotless, mature, righteous and complete. The Spirit of Truth that rested upon Him was the source and sustainer of these qualities of perfection, which kept Him free of iniquity. Begin to visualize what your life would look like with these same qualities and pray about what changes you need to make in your life in order to see this come to pass.

Chapter 12

Iniquity and the Kingdom of Heaven

> "The doctrine of the Kingdom of Heaven, which was the main teaching of Jesus, is certainly one of the most revolutionary doctrines that ever stirred and changed human thought." – H.G. Wells

In Matthew, Chapter 7, verse 23, Jesus stated, "And then will I profess unto them, I never knew you: depart from me, ye that work iniquity" (KJV). This scripture was already discussed in a previous chapter, but we will revisit it here. Notice that Jesus did not say "ye that work sin."

His statement "I never knew you" is meant in the context of, "I never had a relationship with you." Someone can have knowledge of God and even practice a religion but still be cut off from a true Kingdom-of-God relationship and experience. The deceptive power of iniquity severs a true relationship with God and keeps Christians from being able to further the Kingdom of Heaven.

Satan has no problem with someone being "religious" according to manmade philosophies, traditions and doctrines [Col. 2:8]. What Satan does have a problem with—what he will try to keep you from every day of your Christian life—is understanding and applying the Word of truth pertaining to the true Kingdom of God [See Matt. 13:19, Mark 4:15, Luke 8:20].

In reading the Gospels you will notice that the Kingdom of God (also referred to as the Kingdom of Heaven) is a primary subject that Jesus talked about. In fact, one of the primary reasons that He came into this world was that He might reintroduce to humanity what the Kingdom of Heaven was all about, that He might paint the true picture of His Father and His Heavenly Kingdom.

Iniquity keeps us from that true understanding. It is therefore the root cause of all the false religions and beliefs that exist in the world today, including many of the denominations that have deviated from God's original message of His Kingdom.

The mysteries of the Kingdom can only be revealed through the Spirit of Truth. Knowledge that is not founded in truth is simply information and could very well be tainted with error. Such information will either fail to bring sustaining transformation or worse, it will give a false impression of security that one is in right standing with God. The presence of iniquity hinders the voice of the Spirit, because the Spirit speaks the language of the kingdom of Heaven: truth. Truth, if allowed, will always bring freedom and unity; it will expose any false belief. Indicators on whether a denomination or religious belief of any kind is tainted with iniquity is if its practices or doctrine teach any form of exclusion, disunity, bondage, attempts to change the moral laws of God, or the blatant disregard for the sanctity of human life.

The Grip of Iniquity

Satan cannot stand the truth. Since he departed from the way of truth and life, he has sought to bring as many as possible along with him. However, Satan is okay with religion that man has tampered with because it keeps people from understanding God's original plan for the Kingdom of Heaven.

> "He who practices truth comes to the Light so that his works may be revealed, that they exist, having been worked in God" (John 3:21).

Many Christians appear to be delivered from sinful environments and behaviors, yet they fail to be set free from those things internally. One can be delivered from committing the physical act of adultery but internally still struggle with the mindset of an adulterer and therefore not be completely free from it. They take care of the "fruit" of sin but rarely deal with the "root" of sin.

Once again, sin is missing the mark of truth. Iniquity is "being bent." Like a bent arrow, it will always result in failure to hit the center of God's will. The ultimate result of this will be a failure to fulfill Jesus' commandment to further the Kingdom of Heaven on earth.

Many today are beginning to gain a greater understanding of what the Kingdom of God / Kingdom of Heaven was truly meant to be. This vital knowledge of the truth transcends traditional religious teaching and is a start towards building that Kingdom. However, many of these believers still struggle with iniquity's hidden grip on their lives.

What is the Kingdom of Heaven? What does it look like? How is it supposed to affect the lives of Christians today?

What Manner of Man is This?

When the Son of God walked this earth over 2,000 years ago, He began to paint a picture. Every parable was a scene. Every work of His was an outline. Every miracle added a splash of color. Sometimes the stories He told seemed as if they described another world, so unique they were in outlook and perception.

Such was the Father in the story of the "prodigal son." In Jesus' time, fathers expected obedience and service; they executed judgment. They never operated out of society's norms. Yet here was a Father running toward his sinful son, folding him in His embrace, forgiving him even before he asked. This Father was even dancing, inviting everyone to join, rejoicing that His son was found, and bestowing love instead of judgment. It was a completely different picture from what the people of Jesus' time were accustomed to hearing and seeing.

The miracles that were spread abroad, which Jesus performed, caused people to sit up and take notice. He did not conjure them up with black magic and chanting. All He did was look to Heaven, utter a few words of thanks to His Father, speak forth in faith, and it was done. The lame walked, those who had been born blind could suddenly see, the deaf could hear the wind blowing through the trees. The dead—who had stepped over the great divide, the threshold from which no man has power to return—were brought to life. They moved and breathed and walked again on this earth.

"What manner of man is this?" many asked, and only a few recognized the truth of who He really was [Matt. 8:27, Mark 4:41, Luke 8:25].

Today we see through the lens of 2,000 years of world history. All Christians know who He was: the Son of God. This was why He had the power to work the works that He did, because He came from the very Kingdom of Heaven.

With all that He did while on Earth, Christ began to paint us a picture of that Kingdom. It was not a static painting. It was a living, breathing and growing portrait. Before He returned to His Father's eternal Kingdom of Heaven, Jesus gave us instructions on how to build His Kingdom on Earth.

If You Love Me...

What are some of the things Jesus told His disciples to do and be and prepare for? The instructions that He gave to them immediately before His ascent into Heaven are the same mandate to which believers of today are called: furthering the Kingdom of Heaven on Earth:

> "And Jesus came and spake unto them, saying, All power is given unto me in heaven and in earth. Go ye therefore, and teach all nations, baptizing them in the name of the Father, and of the Son, and of the Holy Ghost: Teaching them to observe all things whatsoever I have commanded you: and, lo, I am with you always, even unto the end of the world. Amen" (Matt. 28:18-20, KJV).

> "And he said unto them, Go ye into all the world, and preach the gospel to every creature. He that believeth and is baptized shall be saved; but he that believeth not shall be damned. And these signs shall follow them that believe; In my name shall they cast out devils; they shall speak with new tongues; They shall take up serpents; and if they drink any deadly thing, it shall not hurt them; they shall lay hands on the sick, and they shall recover" (Mark 16:15-18, KJV).

Jesus Christ also gave the admonition to all who love Him: "Feed my sheep."

> "So when they had dined, Jesus saith to Simon Peter, Simon, son of Jonas, lovest thou me more than these? He saith unto him, Yea, Lord; thou knowest that I love thee. He saith unto him, Feed my lambs. He saith to him again the second time, Simon, son of Jonas, lovest thou me? He saith unto him, Yea, Lord; thou knowest that I love thee. He saith unto him, Feed my sheep. He saith unto him the third time, Simon, son of Jonas, lovest thou me? Peter was grieved because he said unto him the third time, Lovest thou me? And he said unto him, Lord, thou knowest all things; thou knowest that I love thee. Jesus saith unto him, Feed my sheep" (John 21:15-17, KJV).

Those who believe in Christ's name are called to keep His commandments, to follow His teachings, to fulfill the last mandate He gave before being taken up into Heaven, which He taught for 40 days prior to His ascension. "To whom He also presented Himself living after His suffering by many infallible proofs, being seen by them through forty days, and speaking of the things pertaining to the kingdom of God" (Acts 1:3).

Those instructions are clear:

Feed My sheep.

Go ye.

Teach all nations.

Preach the Gospel of the Kingdom.

Tale of a Talent

Another parable Jesus told, in which He gives an allegory about the Kingdom of Heaven, makes it clear how He expects Christians to accomplish the task that He has set before them.

"For the kingdom of heaven is like a man traveling to a far country, who called his own servants and delivered his goods to them. And to one he gave five talents, to another two, and to another one, to each according to his own ability; and immediately he went on a journey. Then he who had received the five talents went and traded with them, and made another five talents. And likewise he who had received two gained two more also. But he who had received one went and dug in the ground, and hid his lord's money. After a long time the lord of those servants came and settled accounts with them.

"So he who had received five talents came and brought five other talents, saying, 'Lord, you delivered to me five talents; look, I have gained five more talents besides them.' His lord said to him, 'Well done, good and faithful servant; you were faithful over a few things, I will make you ruler over many things. Enter into the joy of your lord.' He also who had received two talents came and said, 'Lord, you delivered to me two talents; look, I have gained two more talents besides them.' His lord said to him, 'Well done, good and faithful servant; you have been faithful over a few things, I will make you ruler over many things. Enter into the joy of your lord.'

> *"Then he who had received the one talent came and said, 'Lord, I knew you to be a hard man, reaping where you have not sown, and gathering where you have not scattered seed. And I was afraid, and went and hid your talent in the ground. Look, there you have what is yours.'*
>
> *"But his lord answered and said to him, 'You wicked and lazy servant, you knew that I reap where I have not sown, and gather where I have not scattered seed. So you ought to have deposited my money with the bankers, and at my coming I would have received back my own with interest. Therefore take the talent from him, and give it to him who has ten talents"* (Matt. 25:14-28).

With that story, Christ makes it clear that whether a believer knows much or little, whether they are very gifted or have only one gift—or talent—there is a single purpose for that one gift: to further the Kingdom of Heaven. When we are faithful to do so, we will hear the words: "Well done, thou good and faithful servant."

When we are not faithful to do so, when we bury the talent or hide it beneath a life of selfish pursuits—or even a life of good works, yet not the works that God has ordained—we will find that the rewards He bestows depend on our faithfulness to the works He has called us to accomplish for Him.

The words He spoke to the servant who buried His talent: "You wicked and lazy servant," might seem rather harsh, leaving one to think, "Is that really fair? After all, he only had one talent. He was just trying to keep it safe."

In Bible times, one "talent" would take the average working man over 23 years to earn. The equivalent today would be—for someone working a normal eight-hour day five days a week at, let's say, $10 an hour—nearly $500,000 gross income.

What would you do with five hundred thousand dollars? What would you do if you had five times that amount? Or ten times? When thinking about having such a huge sum of money, the mind automatically starts to become energetic and plans begin to form.

Buy a house. Start a business. Open a school. Give to missions. Some causes could be noble. Some could be selfish. Some could be a mixture of both. Yet even the most unselfish cause in the world, *if it was not God's plan*, would be the equivalent of burying that talent, taking a box and stashing $500,000 in there, digging a hole in the backyard and leaving it there awaiting the King's return.

It's easy to say, "Well of course I wouldn't bury it! That's a lot of money!" Can you say the same for the unique talents and gifts God has given you for the purpose of furthering His Kingdom of Heaven on Earth? He hasn't given you mere money that will pass away, or that inflation will come along and make it worthless. The talents and gifts you have are directly from God, which He has given to you and you alone. Each gift is bestowed from Heaven and is worth more than any amount of money in this world, for "the world passes away . . . but he that does the will of God abides forever."

Let's say, for instance, a Christian's unique, God-given talent is singing. It would be easy for that individual to say, "Well, there are a thousand great singers. There are wonderful singers in the church choirs. There are amazing singers and writers that have started bands. Some songs have brought many to Christ. What difference would I make? My voice isn't that great compared to many. It might be good, but what difference does my single voice make?"

The Great Symphony

There is a story told of a clarinet player who was a member in a large orchestra. Hundreds of other musicians were there with their musical instruments—flutes and oboes, violins and cellos, organs and harps. Woodwinds, strings, percussion, brass; all joined together in one grand symphony. During practice, the clarinet player heard all the others playing their parts and his part seemed so infinitesimal compared to all the others. He assumed that he did not make the slightest difference in the symphony and he decided not to play. It was time for the final practice, right before the crowds began to arrive. The musicians took their places, the conductor lifted his baton, and the music began.

Symbols clashed, cellos vibrated, mesmerizing violin notes weaved among the other parts, but suddenly, everything stopped. The conductor had commanded the music to cease and it ended, mid-note.

"Where is the clarinet player?" he demanded, not unkindly. The man stood quietly, inwardly cringing.

"I…"

"You didn't play your part," the conductor observed.

"I didn't think…" he stumbled and fell silent in embarrassment.

Somehow, the conductor knew what the problem was. Rather than pressing the issue, he smiled and said, "Every part is important and needs to be played, whether small or great, whether one line or 20 on these sheets of music."

With that, the conductor lifted his baton once more and the orchestra played their symphony, complete this time, with the soft, gentle sound of the clarinet coming through at the time it was needed.

God is the Master Orchestrator. He conducts the symphony of what is currently over seven billion lives, weaving them in and out in perfect precision, having a specific plan, a perfect part for each one of them to play. He knows when we play it, and He smiles. He also knows when we do not, when we fail—perhaps from lack of faith, perhaps from lack of desperation in seeking Him for His plan, perhaps from lack of belief that there even is a plan. There is a plan, a beautiful symphony that is incomplete without you playing your part, as humble as it might be.

To continue with the example of the Christian whose talent is singing; yes, perhaps that individual will never start up a band and grow famous. Maybe he or she will never even sing for more than a few people at a time. Perhaps that voice, and the message conveyed in the words that are sung, will touch the heart of one person . . . and that person will bring one other person to Christ . . . and that was their purpose. Not one thousand, but one. If it is their calling, then it is better to sing for that one person than to sing before millions. That is fulfilling one's calling, a God-given purpose that is furthering the Kingdom of Heaven.

In the symphony of the church today, we have those who are called to play the flute rushing off to clash some symbols. We have those who are ordained to play the cello instead screeching out notes on a violin. We have those who are called to sing solo sitting off on the sidelines not realizing they even have a part to play.

The beautiful picture—the portrait of the Kingdom of Heaven that Jesus began to paint so perfectly while He was on earth—stands there, virtually untouched. A few splashes of color here, a few dark lines of impressions there, but for the most part it has not become the picture that He ordained it to be. What's more, when those who have called themselves Christians live a purpose other than that for which they have been created, the picture is marred, and the effect on other's perception of the Kingdom of Heaven is negatively affected.

It is almost as if a four-year-old child has gotten a hold of one of Monet's paintings and begun to paint over the perfect masterpiece with watercolors. When we follow our own design, when we follow after iniquity rather than pursuing our God-given purpose, we are that child with the watercolors, perhaps happy and gleeful and full of color, but in reality, all we make is a big mess.

But all is not lost. It is not hopeless. The blood of Christ can wash over that portrait, washing away the stains and marks, even of thousands of years, making it clean and perfect again. However, we must not take up the brush in our own hands again, seeking to paint a picture that *we* feel is lovely and wonderful. We must let *Him* hold the brush of our lives and use the colors that He wishes and the strokes that He chooses to create—not our picture, but God's.

That will be the only way that the true picture of the Kingdom of God can be painted, on earth, as it is in Heaven.

⌘

Chapter Summary:

- Someone can have knowledge of God and even practice a religion but still be cut off from a true Kingdom-of-God relationship and experience.

- The deceptive power of iniquity severs a true relationship with God and keeps Christians from being able to further the Kingdom of Heaven.

- Satan has no problem with someone being "religious" according to manmade philosophies, traditions and doctrines. He will try to keep you from understanding and applying the Word of truth pertaining to the true Kingdom of God.

- Iniquity is the root cause of all the false religions and beliefs that exist in the world today, including many of the denominations that have deviated from God's original message of His Kingdom.

- The Kingdom of God (also referred to as the Kingdom of Heaven) is a primary subject that Jesus talked about; it is one of the primary reasons that He came into this world.

- You have a special place within the Kingdom of God and are given a unique role to fulfill, as well as the talents and gifts you need to fulfill that role.

APPLICATION:

1. Take an honest assessment of your life and ask yourself if you have been guilty of being "religious" according to manmade philosophies, traditions and doctrines of men rather than following the pure unadulterated Word of truth pertaining to the Kingdom of God.

2. Reflect on the talents and gifts that you have been given by God. Have you sought Him about what those talents and gifts are, and how you can begin to use them to further the Kingdom of God on earth? Are you using them for His glory?

Chapter 13

THE BLOOD, THE WATER AND THE SPIRIT

"The greatest peace treaty that has ever been established on the earth is the agreement between the Blood, the Water, and the Spirit." – Julio Alvarado Jr.

Throughout this book we have looked at the cancer of iniquity through its two streams. One stream is the biological transfer through the male's physical loins. The other stream of iniquity is conceived and birthed through the loins of the mind by the rejection of the Spirit of Truth [Hosea 4:1, 6; John 16:13]. Whether iniquity is transferred biologically—through a natural father—or is present due to the obstruction of truth from God in Heaven, the good news is that there is a remedy to rid oneself of iniquity.

If you claim to have Christ in your life, the cancer of iniquity has to be removed. Some forms of natural cancer are untreatable and eventually lead to a premature death. All forms of the cancer of iniquity—spiritual and biological—are not only treatable but must be removed. The consequence of not removing iniquity from your life is the present and eternal rejection of God, portrayed through Jesus' statement below:

"Not everyone that saith unto me, Lord, Lord, shall enter into the kingdom of heaven; **but he that doeth the will of my Father which is in heaven.** *Many will say to me in that day, Lord, Lord, have*

we not prophesied in thy name? And in thy name have cast out devils? And in thy name done many wonderful works? And then will I profess unto them, **I never knew you: depart from me, ye that work iniquity"** *(Matt. 7:21-23, KJV).*

Old Testament Remedy for Iniquity

In order to gain a complete perspective and understanding of the iniquity removal process, we have to take an in-depth look at how God instructed His people to remove iniquity and its effects in the past. In Chapter 16 of Leviticus, we can read that God gave Moses specific, detailed instructions to the priests in how to deal with the wrongdoings of the people. The priests represented the people to God and He gave them a number of ceremonies to perform in order to be cleansed of iniquities, sins and transgressions.

I encourage you to read the entire 16th chapter of Leviticus to get the full essence of these crucial ceremonies. This particular chapter is foundational to the removal process of sin and transgression, and their root cause—iniquity. It is important to examine this chapter in order to extract the key principles in this chapter that are a type, or shadow, of today's removal process for iniquity.

These instructions were given to Moses after two of Aaron's sons, Nadab and Abihu, (who were also priests) were slain by God due to their "iniquitized" disobedience. They offered sacrifices that were not commissioned of God, an act that is figurative of people today who decide how *they* want to serve God instead of following *God's* specific instructions.

In the chapter, God went on to give Moses instructions for the priests, who represented the people of Israel to God. He relayed the method to deal with iniquity. Aaron, Moses' brother, who was the high priest at that time, performed this ceremony of sacrifice for the atonement of the people once a year.

> "And Aaron shall lay both his hands upon the head of the live goat, and confess over him all the iniquities of the children of Israel, and all their transgressions in all their sins, putting them upon the head of the goat, and shall send him away by the hand of a fit man into the wilderness: And the goat shall bear upon him all their iniquities unto a land not inhabited: and he shall let go the goat in the wilderness" (Lev. 16:21-22).

We have already defined iniquity and sin. At this point it is also important to define "transgressions," which is the same word as the more commonly used word "trespasses." The Hebrew word for both transgression and trespass is *pesha*, which is "rebellion that is physically acted out." Transgression is missing the mark (sin) through a physical act of your body due to some form of rebellion that is rooted in iniquity.

This ceremonial process was to be used not only for the removal of iniquity but also for the removal of transgressions and sins. Aaron would lay his hand on the head of the live goat and confess all the people's iniquities, transgressions and sins. This process is where we get the term "scapegoat." Before Christ's sacrifice, the shedding of blood from animals was required for the atonement of sins; only the high priest could perform this crucial ceremony. The principle of this process still applies today: Jesus made the ultimate sacrifice and anyone who claims the cleansing power of His blood receives remission of sin [See Heb. 2:17, 3:1, 4:14-15, 5:10, 6:20, 7:26, 8:1, 9:11, 9:25].

> "Unto you first God, having raised up his Son Jesus, sent him to bless you, in turning away every one of you from his iniquities" (Acts 3:26, KJV).

In the Old Testament, this ceremony had to be performed once a year in order for the removal of iniquities, transgressions and sins. This vital process was an outline or type of what later took place at Calvary through the crucifixion and sacrifice of the blood of our High Priest, Jesus Christ. As a result of Jesus' sacrifice, animal blood is no longer required, nor is it valid. Humanity now has access to a perfect (mature, complete, whole) state of being through the sacrifice of the Son of God [See Eph. 4:13, Phil. 3:15, Col. 1:28, 2 Tim. 3:17, 1 Pet. 5:10].

> "For the Law which has a shadow of good things to come, not the very image of the things, appearing year by year with the same sacrifices, which they offer continually, they are never able to perfect those drawing near" (Heb. 10:1).

In Leviticus 16:2-4 we read that Aaron could not perform this ceremony in his normal state. He had to prepare himself by sacrificing specified animals and dressing himself in a certain way according to the instructions of God. If he had not followed the instructions, he would most likely have also experienced an untimely death, similar to his two sons.

> "And the LORD said unto Moses, Speak unto Aaron thy brother, that he come not at all times into the holy place within the vail before the mercy seat, which is upon the ark; **that he die not**: for I will appear in the cloud upon the mercy seat.

> "Thus shall Aaron come into the holy place: with a young bullock for a sin offering, and a ram for a burnt offering.

> "He shall put on the holy linen coat, and he shall have the linen breeches upon his flesh, and shall be girded with a linen girdle, and with the linen mitre shall he be attired: these are holy garments; therefore shall **he wash his flesh in water**, and so put them on" (Lev. 16:2-4).

These instructions came from the mouth of God. That which comes from the mouth of God is always truth, which literally becomes a law unto you. The ultimate purpose of this law is to bring some type of order into your life. Words from the mouth of God literally become scripture for you and will always fall under the topic of teaching, correcting or some other type of instruction. It will always encourage you to develop in the understanding of God's plan for your life or help you grow in righteousness and spiritual maturity [2 Tim. 3:16].

God will always give you the power of truth that will come in the form of instructions in order to create or reproduce His purposes.

Truth has two primary functions:

#1: To nurture or feed the covenant that God has with you so that you may have an unhindered relationship with God, enabling Him to provide information to help you create or reproduce His will.

#2: To cleanse you from sin, transgression, rebellion or any other form of wrong that is rooted in iniquity, which is what keeps you from experiencing God's creative power in your life.

A remedy from all that is wrong in life can always be found in the Word of God.

Three Essential Elements

Though there were many things that had to be done to perform this important ceremony, three key elements were crucial in order to perform it accurately.

The first crucial element was **"truth"**—the detailed instructions that came from the mouth of God.

The second key element was **"blood"**—the sacrifice and blood of specific animals.

The third essential element was clean **"water"**—which had to be used to cleanse the garments and flesh of the high priest who was to perform this crucial ceremony.

These three elements are a type, or shadow, of the three crucial elements needed today in order to remove any manifestations of iniquity.

The following portion of scripture gives us insight as to who first discovered, witnessed and dealt with the iniquity of Lucifer in Heaven. [Again, Lucifer's iniquity is covered in Ezekiel 28:15.]

> *"For there are three that bear witness in heaven: the Father, the Word, and the Holy Spirit, and these three are one"* (1 John 5:7).

"The Word" in this passage is a reference to Jesus before He was birthed on the earth [John 1:1-2, 14]. A witness is one that provides facts that validate one's innocence or guilt, based off evidence that they have seen themselves or of which they have knowledge.

The triune Godhead discovered, witnessed and dealt with Lucifer's iniquitized condition in Heaven. Jesus is now the full essence of this Godhead according to Colossians, Chapter 2, verse 9, which states, "For in Him dwells all the fullness of the Godhead bodily."

Jesus is still in the business of discovering and being a witness against any form of iniquity within a human being. Jesus provided and introduced a triune remedy for iniquity that, if permitted to go to work in your life, will help you to discover and root out iniquity.

In the following scripture we see that Jesus reintroduced into the earth the three crucial key elements that we find in Leviticus Chapter 16. These elements must be properly understood and appropriated in order to root out iniquity from one's life.

> *"This is he that came by water and blood, even Jesus Christ; not by water only, but by **water** and **blood**. And it is the Spirit that beareth witness, because **the Spirit is truth**"* (1 John 5:6, KJV).

The crucifixion of Jesus literally poured these three elements upon the earth. When Jesus uttered His last words on the cross and gave up the ghost [Mark 15:37, 39], His blood and water were shed: "But when they came to Jesus and saw that He was already dead, they did not break His legs. But one of the soldiers pierced His side with a lance, and instantly there came out blood and water" (John 19:33-34).

On the cross, Jesus released the three key elements from His body that must be properly appropriated, understood and applied in order to fully apply the remedy of iniquity and not take the sacrifice of His life in vain. There was a clear manifestation of Jesus releasing His spirit as well as the distinction of both water and blood. Again, these are symbolic and a type of the three key elements needed to root out iniquity that we see in Leviticus 16.

Jesus had to release His Spirit so that we can have access to the Holy Spirit [John 14:26, 15:26 and 16:17].

> "And crying with a loud voice, Jesus said, Father, into Your hands I commit My spirit. And when He had said this, He breathed out the spirit" (Luke 23:46).

The Blood

Jesus provided His natural blood, which we need to spiritually apply to our lives. His blood came directly from God the Father. As such, it was free from any "iniquitized" male influence. John the Baptist, the forerunner of Jesus, said that Jesus was the one who takes away the sin of the world [John 1:29]. This sacrifice required the shedding of His blood, the taking of His life.

During what is traditionally known as The Last Supper, Jesus said, "For this is My blood of the new covenant, which is shed for many for the remission [or forgiveness] of sins" (Matt. 26:28).

Jesus also made some very interesting and controversial statements to His followers and to the religious people of His day about His blood. When Jesus made the following statements about drinking His blood, those listening assumed a literal application of His statements, which they took to mean that they would literally have to drink His blood.

> "Then Jesus says to them, 'Truly, truly, I say to you, Unless you eat the flesh of the Son of Man, and drink His blood, you do not

have life in yourselves. Whoever partakes of My flesh and drinks My blood has eternal life, and I will raise him up at the last day. For My flesh is food indeed, and My blood is drink indeed. He who partakes of My flesh and drinks My blood dwells in Me, and I in him'" (John 6:53-56).

The term "eat the flesh of the Son of Man" is connected to another statement that Jesus made about Himself, when He stated that He was "the bread of life" that came down from Heaven [John 6:34-35, 48, 51]. The word flesh is *basar*. It is defined as "the skin and muscle or the whole of the person." In the *Ancient Hebrew Lexicon of the Bible*, *basar* is also defined as "someone who brings good news," which is the definition for the word *gospel*. When Jesus made statements about the need to "eat His flesh," what He was literally saying was *"eat my gospel."* His statement was not some type of cannibalistic announcement that one must eat His natural flesh. Similar to the misunderstanding that Nicodemus the Pharisee had when Jesus shared with him the profound truth that one must be "born again" in order to experience the Kingdom of God, the people who heard Christ's words assumed a natural application instead of the appropriate spiritual application.

When Jesus taught His disciples to pray [Matt. 6:11 and Luke 11:3], the statement "Give us this day our daily bread" was a reference to a daily seeking of the will of God through hearing His words. This becomes the gospel or good news specifically for our lives, which we are then supposed to "flesh out" into our actions and performances. Therefore, to "eat the flesh of the Son of Man" is to consume the *gospel* or *spiritual bread* (the word of truth) that causes us to experience inner growth so that we may learn how to walk in the will and the Spirit of God.

When Jesus referred to eating His body and drinking His blood, He meant that we must spiritually consume that which kept Him free of iniquity. The reason we are instructed to examine ourselves during communion is to make sure that no form of iniquity is present within us.

> "And giving thanks, He broke it and said, 'Take, eat; this is My body, which is broken for you; this do in remembrance of Me.' In the same way He took the cup also, after supping, saying, **This cup is the New Covenant in My blood; as often as you drink it, do this in remembrance of Me.'** For as often as you eat this bread and drink this cup, you show the Lord's death until He shall come.
>
> "So that whoever shall eat this bread and drink this cup of the Lord unworthily, he will be guilty of the body and blood of the Lord. **But let a man examine himself,** and so let him eat of that bread and drink of that cup. For he who eats and drinks unworthily eats and drinks condemnation to himself, not discerning the Lord's body.
>
> "For this cause many among you are weak and sickly, and many sleep" (1 Cor. 11:24-30).

Jesus' life sacrifice took away the sins of the world, but it didn't take away the iniquity of the world. Jesus was bruised for our iniquities, according to Isaiah 53:5. Again, sin is a manifestation of iniquity. Jesus' blood and life sacrifice grants us access to the removal of all sin in our life. Instead of the animal sacrifices that God previously required, all we have to do is confess our sin. However, iniquity is removed by the Spirit of Truth only as we follow its instructions and are therefore cleansed through "the washing of the water of the Word."

> "**Wash** me thoroughly from mine iniquity, and **cleanse** me from my sin" (Ps. 51:2).

> "And I will **cleanse** them from all their iniquity, whereby they have sinned against me; and I will pardon all their iniquities, whereby they have sinned, and whereby they have transgressed against me" (Jer. 33:8).

The blood of Jesus that originated from the seed of God gives us the spiritual blood transfusion that we need. Spiritually, when we appropriate the blood of Jesus accurately into our lives, it should produce what I call the "God Seed," which includes the DNA of

God, which includes the Golgi Apparatus of God [introduced in the Science and Biology of Iniquity chapter].

The purpose of this "Kingdom of God seed" is to provide Kingdom Words from God to supply us with Heavenly information and knowledge. These Kingdom Words are meant to travel to the brain—the loins of the mind—and throughout the vein and nerve systems; if properly appropriated, they will affect the thought process of an individual, recreating them into the likeness and image of God, according to the mind of God.

We find this Kingdom growth principle in the parable of the soils when the seed falls into the good ground [See Matt. 13:1-23, Luke 8:4-15, Mark 4:1-20]. If the seed of the word in this parable comes from Heaven—which is without iniquity—doesn't it make sense that the heart that receives it has to eventually become iniquity free so that it produces the ultimate goal of a hundredfold? I have come to the conclusions that this hundredfold fruit is synonymous with the perfect or mature will of God that is found in Romans Chapter 12, verse 2.

The Spirit of Truth

> *"If we say that we have fellowship with Him and walk in darkness, we lie and do not practice the truth. But if we walk in the light, as He is in the light, we have fellowship with one another, and the blood of Jesus Christ His Son cleanses us from all sin. If we say that we have no sin, we deceive ourselves, and the truth is not in us. If we confess our sins, He is faithful and just to forgive us our sins, and to cleanse us from all unrighteousness. If we say that we have not sinned, we make Him a liar, and His Word is not in us"* (1 John 1:6-10).

In the above passage, "walking in darkness" means to walk in ignorance. Light is a reference to knowledge that is truth-based. Although we can receive truth principles from the Holy Scriptures, it is even more important to learn to accurately and consistently hear the Spirit of Truth when it comes to specific guidance for your life. The voice of God is the most accurate form of truth and is the highest level of "sin revealer" in your life. The voice of God is also a cleansing agent for your life.

Jesus' blood gives us access to the forgiveness of sins, not just as a one-time event but as a daily event... as long as truth is practiced. The conditional word "if," found in the verses above, make it clear that we must confess our sins *and* walk in the light.

The Spirit of Truth, which is the voice of God, will inform you whether or not iniquity is evident in your life. This is why it is so important to learn to hear the voice of God for your life, and to root out all that keeps you from hearing Him accurately. The Holy Spirit will reveal where iniquity is present in your life. The function of the Holy Spirit in this iniquity-removal process is to provide you with information on how to remove iniquity from your life and how to keep it out once it has been removed.

The Water

The Spirit of Truth will reveal areas where you are missing the mark (sinning) in your life. The Spirit of Truth will also function as water in cleansing those areas permanently from your life. The Spirit of Truth has two primary functions: to nurture, or feed, the relationship that God desires to have with you, and to give you information on how to cleanse your life from all forms of iniquity.

The Spirit of Truth gives us the washing that we need through the principles of the *written word* and the more specific water or *spoken word* for our lives, which acts a cleanser. Biblically, this was called *Rhema* in Greek or *Emet* in Hebrew.

> "With what shall a young man **cleanse** his way? By taking heed according to **Your Word**" (Ps. 119:9).

*"That He might sanctify and **cleanse** it with **the washing of water by the Word**" (Eph. 5:26).*

What the Old Testament ceremony foretold, the New Testament sacrifice fulfilled. Through the triune cleansing power of Jesus' water, blood and Spirit, we have free access to the remedy for iniquity. Rather than let His sacrifice be in vain, we must apply the cleansing power of His Spirit, His blood and the water of His word to every area of our lives.

⌘

Chapter Summary:

- Words from the mouth of God literally become scripture for you and will always fall under the topic of teaching, correcting or some other type of instruction.

- Before Jesus' sacrifice, God commanded His people how to perform special ceremonies for the remission of sin and iniquity. When Jesus died on the cross, He fulfilled and took the place of that ceremony.

- Three elements—the blood, the water, and the spirit—are crucial in the process of removing iniquity.

- The Spirit of Truth, which is the voice of God, will inform you whether or not iniquity is evident in your life. This is why it is so important to learn to hear the voice of God for your life, and to root out all that keeps you from hearing Him accurately.

- Whether iniquity is transferred biologically—through a natural father—or is present due to the obstruction of truth from God in Heaven, the good news is that there is a remedy to rid oneself of iniquity.

Application:

1. Reflect on whether you have properly appropriated and applied Jesus' blood, the water, and the Spirit over every area of your life in order to be cleansed and made anew.

2. Now that you have a better understanding of iniquity, begin to make a list of all iniquitized behavior that you have been guilty of. Though this process may be painful, it helps you to get a proper prescription from God on how to root these out of your life. This is similar to diagnostic data or an image that your doctor receives from a test that you have taken; when something is out of order, he can pinpoint and prescribe a specific remedy.

3. Reflect on your ability to hear the voice of God consistently. If you are currently struggling with hearing His voice, what do you believe is hindering this vital experience?

Chapter 14

THE INIQUITY REMOVAL PROCESS

"Truth is the illuminator that exposes iniquity; ignorance is the darkness that keeps iniquity from being seen." – Julio Alvarado Jr.

Though we have access to the removal of iniquity through Jesus' death on the cross, many Christians still suffer from the effects of iniquity and its disastrous consequences. I was one of them. Though I had been delivered from many of my past behaviors and lifestyle and had taken steps to confess and renounce all of my known sin, I still had the virus of iniquity affecting my everyday living without even knowing it.

This past year I had the opportunity to interview my mother and biological father. I hoped to find out about my ancestors in order to research, in my own genealogy, what I had been discovering about iniquity. I asked my parents to give me as much detail that they had knowledge of from the previous four generations, at least. What I discovered shocked me, yet also blessed me. The shock came from hearing that my father, grandfather, great grandfather and even great-great grandfather all suffered from similar behaviors of those things I had a tendency toward. The blessing came in discovering that, as long as I did something about it, I no longer had to be a victim of the biology of my ancestors. I had the power to change the future potential of my family tree.

New Testament Confusion

Many Christians today falsely believe that they are a new complete person as a result of their confession and conversion through a born-again experience. Though this is an important starting point, we have to remember that it is only a first step. It is true that if anyone is in Christ, they are made anew, but there is still a lot of growth before us. We are no longer victims or at the mercy of the sins of our fathers, but we still can suffer the consequences and the effects of their iniquities [Ez. 18:17-26, KJV].

Many diseases today are known to be hereditary. This hereditary transfer passes through the semen, which is also the conduit of iniquity. I believe that many physical diseases are also rooted in the DNA of iniquity, yet the following passage gives us hope for the healing of these diseases.

> "Bless the LORD, O my soul, and forget not all his benefits: Who forgiveth all thine iniquities; who healeth all thy diseases; Who redeemeth thy life from destruction; who crowneth thee with lovingkindness and tender mercies" (Ps. 103:2-4, KJV).

A person who doesn't know that they are sick has no reason to pursue any form of treatment, especially if their body doesn't manifest any symptoms of the sickness. This issue is evident in the lives of many believing Christians today. They believe—and are sometimes even taught—that once they become a born-again believer or simply quote a prayer to accept Christ, they are immune from sinful living, harmful character flaws, and negative patterns of thinking.

Though praying to accept Christ or going through the initial steps of being born again are good starts, they are not the complete cure for iniquity's presence and effects. This is the reason many in the church today still struggle from unhealthy practices such as alcoholism, drug addiction, infidelity, marital problems, homosexuality, lesbianism, financial lack, depression and many other negative behaviors and patterns of thinking. Although they have Christ in their lives, they still have not gained a complete and lasting victory over the things that they were involved in before turning to Christ. As such, it is easy for many to ask, "Where is the power of the cross?" when in reality, Christ's power in our lives is made of none effect through our acceptance of the hidden presence of iniquity.

The following passage confirms that mercy and forgiveness are available from God, yet mercy and forgiveness don't, in themselves, remove iniquity. Iniquity is forgiven—along with transgressions and sins—yet if it is never dealt with properly, the iniquity of the fathers is still visited by the presence of God until it is removed. Iniquity breeds sin and transgressions. Mercy and forgiveness do not remove iniquity completely; truth applied in the life of a believer is what permanently removes iniquity and its effects...as long as that truth is continually applied.

> *"Keeping mercy for thousands, forgiving iniquity and transgression and sin, and that will by no means clear the guilty; visiting the iniquity of the fathers upon the children, and upon the children's children, unto the third and to the fourth generation"* (Ex. 34:7).

Grace Revisited – Grace that Saves

As mentioned before, many confuse the *grace* of God with the *mercy* of God. Grace by itself is not the remedy to man's problems nor is it an excuse for man's sinful and ungodly behavior. Many today justify their shortcomings by claiming God's grace as if it is a "get-out-of-jail-free" card. Grace is a biblical concept, yet many fail to acknowledge or understand the work of *truth* in the justification process. God is merciful in that He has provided a remedy for iniquity. His own Son delivered the remedy for iniquity through His blood [1 John 1:7] and through the provision of grace and truth.

> "And the Word became flesh, and tabernacled among us. And we beheld His glory, the glory as of the only begotten of the Father, **full of grace and of truth**" (John 1:14).

> "For the Law came through Moses, but **grace and truth** came through Jesus Christ" (John 1:17).

Grace and truth cannot be separated. Grace is the portal for receiving truth. Grace is the beautiful nature of God manifested in His kindness and compassion, and His desire to show favor towards mankind through the deliverance of truth. The inseparably linked gifts of grace and truth provide exactly what is needed in order to experience ultimate freedom from sin, transgression, lawlessness and all other forms of disobedience. This provision comes in the form of knowledge and it leads to genuine freedom. It is the application of this provision of knowledge that literally makes one free from the grip of iniquity. Jesus Himself stated this fact in this life-changing statement: "You shall know the truth, and the truth shall make you free" (John 8:32).

The traditional understanding of grace gives a false sense of security that doesn't seek out the voice of truth in our lives, which is what the grace of God is designed and authorized to deliver. When grace is made to stand alone without its connection to truth, a misappropriation of its understanding, purpose and function will occur, the result being that its primary benefit cannot be experienced. Salvation should never be viewed as just a one-time event. It should be experienced every day of our lives.

> "For the grace of God **that brings** salvation **has appeared** to all men, **teaching** us that, having denied ungodliness and worldly lusts, we should live discreetly, righteously and godly, in this present world" (Titus 2:11-12).

Grace is the portal for salvation in that it introduces what one should have faith for that leads to a salvation process. Let's examine this process thoroughly through the following passages of scripture:

> "For by grace you are saved **through** faith, and that not of yourselves, it is the gift of God, not of works, lest anyone should boast. For we are His workmanship, created in Christ Jesus to good works, which God has before ordained that we should walk in them" (Eph. 2:8-10).

It is important to notice the key word "through" in the above passage. Grace is the channel by which we are supposed to experience faith. It is also important to notice that this faith does not originate from us; it is a gift from God. This passage informs us that this process should never be a result of our own works but the works that have been predestined for our lives. In other words, we cannot involve ourselves in good works that *we believe* are right; we must discover the *predestined works* that are right *for us*.

When Jesus uttered the words, "And then will I profess unto them, I never knew you: depart from me, ye that work iniquity" (Matt. 7:23), he was speaking to a group of people whose faith and works had been built in the wrong things, thus they did not experience the grace of God for their lives.

This will bring up the age-old debate that we are not saved by works, but we are saved by simply by grace. As we can clearly see, grace is attached to truth, truth is attached to faith, and faith is attached to works.

> "My brothers, what profit is it if a man says he has faith and does not have works? Can faith save him? If a brother or sister is naked and destitute of daily food, and if one of you says to them, Go in peace, be warmed and filled, but you do not give them those things which are needful to the body, what good is it? Even so, **if it does not have works, faith is dead, being by itself.** But someone will say, You have faith, and I have works. Show me your faith without your works, and **I will show you my faith from my works**" (James 2:14-16).

The Spirit of Truth will activate grace in our lives, which teaches us to deny what is ungodly and educates us about what we should have faith in. This process of mentoring leads towards righteous living based off of the reference point of the Kingdom of Heaven rather than the reference point of the traditional religious doctrine of grace, which I believe contaminates the original understanding of the salvation process.

Let's further our understanding of the salvation process by examining the key word "saved." In Ephesians, Chapter 2 verse 8, we read, "For by grace you are saved through faith." The word saved in this verse is the Greek word *sōzo*, which is defined as "to deliver, to preserve, to preserve, to heal, to be made whole." The Hebrew word for saved used in this verse is the word *châyâh*, which is defined as "to relive, to revive, recover, repair and restore."

What is interesting about this Hebrew definition is the use of the prefix "re," which is defined as: "to return to the previous condition." The 4th day (mentioned in chapter 7), in reference to the five "start days," was the day that you decide to become born again. This should begin the process of **re**introducing your original condition, the one that you had before the foundations of the world [Eph. 1:3-5].

To take the word "saved" to a deeper level of understanding, the *Ancient Hebrew Lexicon of the Bible* describes this word as, "Having the *vigor* of life." This definition brings us back to the original definition for iniquity, which as you probably remember is the word "vanity."[23] Jesus Himself used this word—*aven* in Hebrew—in Matthew 7:23, 13:41, 23:28, and 24:12.

Once again, vigor—the opposite of vanity—is defined as "strength, energy or power to produce."[24] Truth is this "power" that we are supposed to use in order to reproduce and create the works that God has preordained for us to do.

Jesus used another form of the word iniquity in the following passage, the Hebrew word *gâ'ôn*, which describes one who is guilty

---

[23] Vanity: The use of the power within the loins for vain or other improper purposes.
[24] Vigor: The power (Truth) within the loins for reproduction or creative work.

of lifting up oneself, which results in wrongful or unrighteous acts. It is also a descriptive definition for the word "pride."

> *"But he shall say, I tell you, I know you not whence ye are; depart from me, all ye workers of iniquity" (Luke 13:27, KJV).*

These unrighteous acts are the works that the grace of God never intended for you to have faith in since they weren't the works that you were saved to do. Those acts were not a part of the original person that God created you to be, and because they weren't founded from the reference point of truth, the result will always be iniquity.

Understanding that the word "saved" means "having the vigor of life" gives the following verse more clarity. Being saved is definitely connected to works and not just a one-time result. It should be an everyday occurrence.

> *"Therefore, my beloved, as you have always obeyed, not as in my presence only, but now much more in my absence, **cultivate your own salvation with fear and trembling.** For it is God **who works in you both to will and to do of His good pleasure**" (Phil. 2:12-13).*

In another book that I have started to write, titled *The Mystery of the Kingdom Revealed*, I give further details about the salvation process. Key components, that are part of the Kingdom of God, lie within every human being. These components in many cases remain dormant in many people and must be discovered, developed and deployed in order for us to properly appropriate the salvation process for our lives.

Your Blood Type

The Spirit of Truth is the grace of God extended to humanity. One of the primary functions of the Holy Spirit is to wash us with the water of the truth of God in order to remove iniquity so that we may function in the fullness of the image and likeness of God.

The blood of Jesus spiritually applied [See 1 John 1:7, Rev. 1:5] is one of the main ingredients necessary to remove iniquity. Physically, when someone has contaminated blood, a blood transfusion of the same blood type is necessary in order for that person's body to recover. Spiritually, we need a blood transfusion from the one and only whose blood type is iniquity free—Jesus' blood—which comes from God Himself. Once you accept Jesus through a born-again experience, you have access to one of the two main ingredients needed to root out iniquity and maintain a life free of its negative effects.

Truth is the other main ingredient, as it is original information from God absent from any trace of iniquity. Truth is what nurtures His covenant with you and delivers all that you need to be whole, complete and free. Truth is the continual "de-iniquitizer" of life. When God speaks to you, His words become law unto you. I believe that this is one of the reasons some people fail to hear from God today. God has spoken to them at some point in their past and they failed to follow that "law" of instruction. In a gesture of love, God stops speaking to that individual to protect him or her from continual disobedience to His other laws of instruction, which would cause that individual to be guilty of further violations against His will. I was guilty of this myself.

The Hebrew word for law is the word *torah*, the root definition of which is "what creates order." One of the primary functions of truth is bringing order to something that is in disarray. This is similar to a doctor prescribing a medication or treatment for something that is not properly functioning and is therefore out of "order" in your body.

Truth that is properly taken and applied will always bring wholeness, peace and health to your spirit, soul and body [1 Thess. 5:23].

Our Fitness Trainer

"The most effective piece of exercise equipment that I have ever used is called DISCIPLINE!" – Julio Alvarado Jr.

God prescribes truth for every aspect of our lives, even down to what we should eat and how we should physically take care of our bodies. If allowed and called upon, the Holy Spirit can become a personal trainer and dietician. Biblically, many types of food were unlawful to eat, including specific types of animals and sea foods.

"Remove far from me vanity and lies: give me neither poverty nor riches; feed me with food convenient for me" (Prov. 30:8, KJV).

The Hebrew word for "convenient" in the passage above is the word *chôq*, defined as, "what is lawful, appointed or prescribed." Today, scientists and doctors are warning of the dangers of fast foods and foods found in groceries stores that contain additives and preservatives, including genetically altered hormones that much of our food sources are given in order to produce them faster. The human body is not designed to process these manmade alterations currently found in much of our food and drink supplies. The convenience of such foods and drinks are the cause of many health issues, including the rise in obesity in children and adults.

The Apostle Paul made numerous key statements pertaining to food and drink when confronted by those that were debating whether foods that had been unlawful to eat were now permitted to eat after Jesus' sacrifice on the cross.

In one of these discussions pertaining to food, Paul made a profound two-part statement in which he stated, "For the kingdom of God is not eating and drinking, but righteousness and peace and joy in the Holy Spirit" (Rom. 14:17). Many have used this passage and others that Paul made about food to validate that is perfectly fine to eat whatever you like.

Though the requirements of the law pertaining to food are no longer in effect today, the principles or spirit of the law still apply today. One reason why many of these foods—such as pork, shrimp, lobster and crab, just to name a few—were unlawful to eat was because of their purpose. All of the above foods were designed by God to eat waste, including the feces of others like themselves. These foods contain parasites that the human body is not designed to consume. The truth about pork and these particular sea foods is that they are garbage disposals designed by God to clean the environments in which they live. Yet these foods are still consumed by millions of people worldwide.

When we fail to understand the truth of something, we will always abuse it. We can become guilty of putting even our diets under a misappropriation of grace. In another one of Paul's discourses that included the topic of food, he stated:

> "'I have the right to do anything,' you say—but not everything is beneficial. I have the right to do anything—but I will not be mastered by anything" (1 Cor. 6:12, NIV).

You may be wondering what food or diet has to do with iniquity? Gluttony is a sin that is rooted in iniquity, but is rarely mentioned. The word gluttony means one who is "loose or undisciplined in eating or drinking excessively." Although believers have the God-given right to enjoy the things that God has created, at the same time, they should be some of the most disciplined people in the world in all facets of their lives, including eating and drinking. Being overweight or unhealthy due to unwise food and beverage choices and portions is not properly representing God.

Unfortunately, it is a common sight today to see ministers who physically express an undisciplined lifestyle of being overweight and in some cases suffering from other health issues due to their dietary choices. A friend of mine had a nephew that he was constantly encouraging to attend church. This nephew disciplined himself in his diet and exercise programs. He put a priority on the value of being in great shape physically. In response to one of these invitations to attend church, he said, "I don't know much about the Bible but I do know that it talks about being disciplined. So why should I go to place where they don't practice what they preach? Look at how overweight you are and how overweight your pastor is."

This young man had a valid point and a proper perspective of the physical condition of many believers today. The sin of gluttony is being allowed to reign free in the body of Christ, when believers should be the most disciplined group of people in the world today.

A Fresh Perspective on the Word "Scripture"

The blood of Jesus is the antidote to iniquity, and truth is the continual scriptural prescription for removing iniquity, which we can receive daily by taking dosages of the written Word and verbal Word through the Spirit of Truth. We will be led to righteousness through the teaching, conviction, correction and instruction of the Holy Spirit, being empowered to perform the good works that we are predestined to do.

> *"All scripture is given by inspiration of God, and is profitable for doctrine, for reproof, for correction, for instruction in righteousness: That the man of God may be perfect, thoroughly furnished unto all good works"* (2 Tim. 3:16-17).

Though the reference in the above passage to "all scripture" is traditionally taught to mean the written Word of God—the Bible—let me introduce a fresh perspective to the meaning of "all scripture." The Hebrew root word for scripture is *kâthâb*, which means both "something written" as well as "the act of writing." When we take the time to listen to and record daily instructions from God, as He lets us know His will for our lives, this "something written" is the scripture for your personal life. When you take time to hear from God, He leads you according to the book that He has already written about you "before the foundations of the earth" [See Ps. 139:16, Jer. 30:2].

Hosea Chapter 4, verse 6 reminds us that God's people were being destroyed for a lack and rejection of knowledge. The word destroyed in this passage is the Hebrew word *dâmâh*, which means to "perceive something as something else." It is a sobering realization that the presence of iniquity has the ability to distort our understanding of the written Word of God. This is more prevalent in the world today than we might care to admit. An example would be using the grace of God as an excuse or license to sin. If one's knowledge of God is distorted because of iniquity, the result will be a perverted view and understanding of God [2 Sam. 22:24-27].

When I began to discover the areas of my life that were infected and affected by iniquity—both naturally and spiritually—I was desperate to get truth straight from God's Spirit in order to rid myself of this spiritual cancer. I started to ask God the right questions so that I could get the right answers. As an example, I no longer justified the existence of sexual lust in my heart as a normal part of me. I determined to stop believing the lies of, "Well, I'm just human," or "I'm a man so God understands," or "As long as I don't physically act it out, I'm ok."

Instead, I began to ask, "Lord, how do I root this lust out of my heart?" His answers came in the form of showing me root causes that I first had to understand and then steps of action that I had to apply in order to not just *remove* it from my heart, but to *keep it out* of my heart.

An example of this was when I realized that the times my wife and I were not getting along or when I felt as though she was not satisfying my sexual drive, my mind would begin to open the door to fantasizing about other women and replaying sexual encounters that I had in the past. My eyes would wander when I saw an attractive women; I would make sure that I got as much of "elevator looking" as I possibly could get. Sometimes I would even get stuck on the middle floors, if you know what I mean.

Once I was aware of this, I had to be on guard during seasons of discontentment in my marriage and seek God for a whole new skill set of thinking and actions in dealing with it. Even though I was a born-again believer, and I had been delivered from the environments of my past sexual activity, the reality hit me that I was not completely set free from it. Truth literally set me free—truth that came from the mouth of God. He began to tell me how to think and act in this situation, as well as in other negative and sinful situations. This process of renewing led me to love and appreciate my wife like never before; it caused me to love her for who she was, not based off of her performance in relation to my selfish and ungodly desires.

I also began to understand that much of my discontentment and dissatisfaction in my marriage was rooted in my failure to be a real man, one that truly functioned in the image and likeness of God through Christ. I was functioning as a mere male with old-nature thinking and behaviors rooted in self-conceived iniquity. My mission in my marriage is now to show my wife the most accurate man that she has ever seen—which should be the goal of every husband towards his wife.

The Fear of the Lord

"Your reverence for God will determine your revelation of God." – Julio Alvarado Jr.

Another main ingredient in the process of removing iniquity is understanding and applying the vital process of "the fear of the

Lord." God has given us access to His mercy as well as to the Holy Spirit of Truth, yet the principle of "the fear of the Lord" also has to be applied.

> "By mercy and truth iniquity is purged: and by the fear of the LORD men depart from evil" (Prov. 16:6).

The word "fear" in this passage is the Hebrew word *yir'âh*, which means "to reverence or respect" someone or something—in this case, the Lord. This same word according to the *Ancient Hebrew Lexicon of the Bible* also means, "A throwing of the finger to show a direction to walk or live or teaching the direction one is to take in life." In other words, we reverence and respect God by allowing Him to "point His finger" and show us the direction to walk and live. This gives the term "the fear of the Lord" much more meaning than what is traditionally taught. Biblically, we see the fear of the Lord defined with the following verse.

> "The fear of the LORD is to hate evil: pride, and arrogancy, and the evil way, and the froward (perverse) mouth, do I hate" (Prov. 8:13, KJV).

The word evil defined here is, "Anything that is dysfunctional or wrong." Pride is defined as "lifting one's own self will." Arrogance is an elevated form of pride and is defined as "swelling one's own soul by making himself his life source." The term "the evil way" is simply defined as, "pursuing the way that is contrary to God's." The "froward or perverse mouth" is speaking anything that goes against truth.

Many believers today have lost focus of—or in some cases have never been accurately taught—the principle or law of "the fear of the Lord," yet it was a foundational principle that navigated Jesus' life on earth [Isa. 11:2-3]. When one truly reverences and respects God at this level, evil, pride, arrogance and false speaking will disappear in the presence of the fear of the Lord. As long as iniquity is present, it will feed these ungodly behaviors, causing God's mercy and truth to be null and void in one's life.

As mentioned before, the blood of Jesus did not contain the human transfer of iniquity since the seed that conceived Him came directly from God through the Holy Spirit [Matt. 1:18, 20]. Jesus was the human form of the male lamb [1 Pet. 1:19, John 1:29] that could not contain blemishes that was used by the Israelites in order for the spirit of the Lord to "pass over" them. (This was so they would not be affected by the 10th plague that God put upon the Pharaoh and the Egyptian people, in which the firstborn son of every family was killed [Ex. 12:1-29].) The Israelites overcame death by the blood of the lamb through the testimony of God's clear instructions, a "type" of what we see in the following passage.

"And they overcame him by the blood of the Lamb, and by the word of their testimony; and they loved not their lives unto the death" (Rev. 12:11, KJV).

Pleading the "blood of Jesus" is a traditional religious saying and is used often in prayer. To verbally plead the blood is not good enough; we have to accept the blood of Jesus not only *over* but also *into* our lives through obedience to God's detailed and individual instructions. Only this will effectively aid the iniquity removal process in our lives. The power and benefits of the blood of Jesus is manifested in obedience to truth and not only by a verbal confession.

In the above passage the reference to overcoming "him" is speaking of Satan himself. It is very important to notice that in order to overcome Satan, both the blood of Jesus *and* the word of our testimony is required. We have already talked extensively about the importance of the blood of Jesus in the iniquity-removal process. The other requirement to overcome Satan is "by the word of their testimony." This reference has nothing to do about how one became saved or born again, but that we overcome Satan (or any other negative situation or enemy) through the testimony that comes from God's mouth through the Spirit of Truth.

God created us and He knows all things, including those things that are wrong with us, and He wants us, His creation, to be free from any form of iniquity. Therefore he has given us the remedy for it. We overcome by the blood Jesus shed, which is "uniniquitized" blood, and by the testimony of truth—"uniniquitized" instructions that God has already witnessed about our lives. Together, these will guarantee success if we take the time to listen to His instructions and obey them.

Contaminated blood affects the whole natural body, especially vital organs. Contaminated thinking and ignorance affects the whole spirit of a person, especially those vital areas that connect us with who we are really supposed to be and our knowledge and experience of who God really is. Spiritually, we need clean uncontaminated blood and the word of God to flow through our mind and heart, which affect our thinking, character, and behaviors. God provided His blood through His Son Jesus, which gives us access to the spiritual transfusion that we need to remove the effects of iniquity, both physically and spiritually.

Quiet Time

It is my personal experience and suggestion that one should take a daily internal inventory of themselves to see if there is any trace of iniquity or manifestations of it present in their lives.[25] Though God has provided a remedy for iniquity, we are still responsible to guard against iniquity. This is part of the self denial and "taking up your cross daily" process that Jesus commands all to do.

> "And he said to them all, If any man will come after me, let him deny himself, and take up his cross daily, and follow me" (Luke 9:23).

I wake up early every morning, before I need to start my normal daily activities, to pray in a place free of distractions so that I can clearly hear from God for my day. Since Jesus is our model, if He did it this way [Mark 1:35], I believe professing believers should follow

---

[25] See link provided of sins in Chapter 7, "The Iniquities of You and Me."

His example. During this time, I sometimes ask, "Lord, search me and let me know if iniquity is either present or crouched at the door of my life." If He brings to my memory or simply tells me that there is something that doesn't belong in my heart, I may ask for a process on how to deal with it. It is also a great idea to spend some time with God in focused, unhindered prayer throughout the day if your schedule allows for it, including before bed.

Though prayer can be done throughout the day, I'm mainly focusing here on prayer that is free from distractions, in a position of stillness, where you can take time to be intimate with God to ensure that His voice is heard. Many believers today either don't hear from God or they fail to obey His words if they do; this is the reason that many believers struggle so intensely in their lives. This might sound like a strong statement, but doesn't it make sense that if someone is clearly hearing and obeying the voice and instructions of God, their life would be in order? Many of our prayers are mere wish lists instead of prayers prayed along the lines of God's will for our lives. Jesus never prayed for things like we do today; He prayed along the lines of God's known will for His life.

I cannot express enough the importance of learning to hear the voice of God on a daily basis in the process of rooting out iniquity and remaining free from its grip.[26] Remember: the voice of God is the voice of the Spirit of Truth, and truth is mandatory in the removal of iniquity. I do believe in quoting and even praying Bible passages since it is the written Word of God. However, it is the spoken Word of God that contains the details for your life that only God knows, which you can't find in the Bible. Once this spoken Word is heard applied, it will bring true change.

---

[26] More on this topic will be covered in a book I am presently writing, the working title of which is: *The Mystery of Prayer Revealed*.

The Power of Fasting

> *"Time invested in strategic prayer, coupled with the abstinence of natural nourishments, introduces a spiritual nourishing and appetite that is simply out of this world."* – Julio Alvarado Jr.

Fasting is a discipline that aids in the process of iniquity removal.[27] When God began to reveal to me that I wasn't as close to Him as I originally thought, He instructed me to strategically fast and pray. It was this act that accelerated the removal of iniquity from my life. The entire chapter of Isaiah 58 is dedicated to the topic of fasting, and in verse six we find an outline of some of the main benefits of fasting.

> *"Is not this the fast that I have chosen? To loose the bands of wickedness, to undo the heavy burdens, and to let the oppressed ones go free, and that you break every yoke?"* (Isa. 58:6, KJV).

The phrase "bands of wickedness" is described in the original Hebrew language as "the binding of the hands and feet due to one who has departed from the correct path or way." Iniquity binds; truth frees. Iniquity will always lead one down the wrong path; truth will always lead one down the correct path of life.

The best way to kill a bad habit or addiction is to starve it. Fasting causes the carnal man to be starved of its carnal desires and causes the inner spirit man to be strengthened. Like protein that is needed in order to build natural muscle, fasting is needed to build spiritual muscle. A lifestyle of disciplined prayer and fasting paves the way to experiencing a preordained Kingdom of God life and relationship with God, free from any form of iniquity.

> *"I was also upright before Him,* **and have kept myself from my iniquity.** *And Jehovah rewarded me according to my righteousness, according to my cleanness in His eyes. With the faithful You will show Yourself faithful; with the upright man You will show*

---

[27] The purpose and power of fasting that transcends traditional teaching will be further explored in my next book on prayer.

Yourself upright. With the pure You will show Yourself pure; and **with the perverted You will appear perverse"** (2 Sam. 22:24-27).

Obviously, the responsibility rests on us to keep ourselves free from iniquity. The benefit in this is that we are then considered righteous, a foundational component to Kingdom-of-God living [Rom. 14:17]. It is also important to note that God's faithfulness, uprightness and pureness towards us is dependent on the absence of iniquity in our lives. A major observation that must be noted is found in verse 27: "With the perverted, you will appear perverse."

The presence of iniquity has the potential to pervert or distort our view of God. I can personally testify to this; when I was guilty of iniquity—biologically and spiritually—my view of God was twisted into a warped understanding of Him. I used my *previous* misunderstanding of grace to justify my ungodly thinking and behaviors. I constantly found myself abusing His forgiveness as a result of my "iniquitized" character.

I will never forget the day that God clearly spoke to me in my morning time with Him. He said, "Julio, I want to take you to a place that you have never been before." When I heard these words, I immediately thought that a change was coming—a different job, ministry, church or change in residence. When I asked God where He wanted to take me, His response was, "I want to take you inside of *My* heart." God then let me know that He couldn't take me inside of His heart in the condition that I was in.

I had been a traditional Christian believer for over 19 years, yet that day I felt as though I had just been indicted by a grand jury for a crime that I didn't even know that I had committed. I quickly discovered that much of what I had been living was a lie. I was not living according to the truth that God had available to me. I was living a religious and traditional life that was definitely an improvement from my former lifestyle, but it was still not the type of living that God required of me, and that He requires of every believer. Thus began the process of me asking God for prescriptions to show and tell me what I had to do in order to get into His heart—the place that I thought I was all along.

The presence of iniquity in my life had perverted my understanding of and my relationship with God. That day I began to ask the right questions, such as, "Lord, what must I do to get inside of Your heart?" He responded by beginning to reveal the iniquity in my life and what I had to do to root it out. I must admit that some of things God revealed to me, I had been convicted of before. Instead of dealing with it though, I had either ignored it or justified its existence, which led to my heart being hardened in that issue.

In Living Color

Following is an example of how His truth was applied to root out the iniquity in my life.

In my immediate family, everyone—including myself—has been divorced at least once. One of my family members has been married and divorced three times. Divorce is widespread in my immediate and extended family. Though all the divorces happened for different reasons, each one has been a result of iniquity in that if truth had been applied, not one of these marriages would have ended up in divorce. In my family, divorce is a generational curse that has been accepted as normal and even expected. My first marriage produced two children and a divorce, which was a result of my "iniquitized" behaviors of drug addiction, alcoholism, and adultery. More than these, though, it was the result of my lack of knowing what the true role and function of a husband was supposed to look like.

The concepts of iniquity and truth were nowhere on my mind at that time since I wasn't a believer. I almost went through a second divorce with my wife Ivette due to the presence of iniquity in my life even after I became a born-again believer. Though I had been removed from the practices of alcoholism and drug addiction, I still didn't know the true role of a husband. Shortly after I filed for divorce without any biblical reason, God gave me a truth solution that began a process of not just restoration in my marriage but a love and appreciation for my wife that I never had before. That restoration continues and is added to every day.

God simply spoke to me and instructed me to study the men that Ivette had been exposed to throughout her life. Her father passed away from a heart attack when she was only six years old. Afterwards, her mother dated men that were simply with her for companionship and sex. Her mother eventually surrendered her life to the Lord and through her church she met a man that she married. This man, who now became Ivette's stepfather, ended up being a pedophile that pursued some of the females in my wife's family, including her daughter. This became a family secret that never was rightfully resolved even after Ivette's mother's untimely death.

Ivette lost her virginity to her first boyfriend at the age of 16 and ended up marrying this man at the age of 20 after becoming pregnant from him. Her first husband was an alcoholic and verbally abusive as well. He committed adultery, which eventually led to their divorce. After Ivette was divorced from her first husband, she dated men that were only in the relationship for companionship and sex, without any real interest in marrying her or being a father to her daughter. Some of these men were also verbally and physically abusive. During Ivette's life, she has also been exposed to pastors of churches that dominated and minimized the placement of a woman, abusing their authority when it came to women.

Ivette and I met at a church we both attended and we were married in April of 1993. It should be no surprise that we had problems in our marriage from the very beginning that involved blended family issues, problems with emotional and sexual intimacy, and struggles with finances and good communication.

When God told me to study the men in Ivette's life, we had been married for approximately 13 years. I discovered, after my "study," the reality that I was the worst one out of all of them. Though I wasn't guilty of some of the behaviors that the other male figures in her life were guilty of, the reason that I consider myself to be the worst one was that, out of all them, I had been with Ivette for the longest period of time. Ivette was never exposed to what I call an "accurate man," a man who truly functions according the image and likeness of God.

Using the working definition for this book, I was guilty of not taking the truth of who I was supposed to be in order to create and reproduce the most accurate husband that I had the potential to be.[28]

Once I discovered the male inaccuracies to which she had been a victim—including my own—God began to give me a truth process. He told me what I needed to do and my obedience to His instruction has resulted in rooting out the character, behaviors and ignorance that were contaminating my marriage. I set a goal to doing whatever I had to do to acquire the knowledge and skills that would enable me to be the most accurate man that Ivette has ever seen. I am so thankful to say that we share a loving, healthy and holy marriage today.

Holy, Pure and Perfect

God is holy, pure and perfect. One of the most profound yet misunderstood mandates that came out of the mouth of Jesus was, "Therefore be perfect, even as your Father in Heaven is perfect" (Matt 5:48). The Hebrew word for perfect is *tâmıym*, which we defined in a prior chapter.[29] In this particular verse, the word perfect is also

---

[28] Spiritual iniquity: To take the power of truth within the loins of the mind and, rather than using it for its intended creative or reproductive work, to instead use it for vain or other improper purposes.

[29] Chapter 7: "The Iniquities of You and Me"

linked to the Hebrew word *shalem*, which is defined as: "to be made whole or complete by adding or subtracting." In other words, we perfect ourselves by adding to our lives those things that make us more like God the Father, and subtracting those things that are not like Him. It is IMPOSSIBLE to accomplish this if iniquity is present in our lives, since God does not have even a trace of iniquity [Deut. 32:4, KJV].

In order to approach and experience God in His pure and perfect state of being, we must be free of iniquity. Many today will say that this is impossible, claiming something akin to, "We all make mistakes" or "We are simply imperfect humans." These are lies that I also used to believe! This is reasoning similar to what Satan, in the form of a serpent, used to introduce iniquity into this world when he twisted the words of God to Eve [Gen. 3:1-5].

God requires every human to be perfect and holy, which must result in a pureness that is absent of any form of iniquity. Holiness has nothing to do with denominational standards such as a uniform dress code, the recommended length of hair, whether or not someone should wear make-up or jewelry, or what public places one can or cannot go to.

It would be unfair for God to require us to be perfect (according to the biblical understanding of perfect) and holy like He is if it were not possible. Holiness is God's nature, which we have the ability to share with Him as long as iniquity is not present in our lives. [Matt: 5:48, 1 Pet. 1:15-16] God is without a spot, blemish or even a wrinkle of iniquity; He requires that His church and people be the same.

Holiness *is not about* what we put on or take off physically; it's the very nature of God. To "be perfect" is about what we put on and take off mentally and spiritually; it's the very essence of what God is. Unfortunately, this is a level of God consciousness, likeness and application that too few people experience due to the deceptive presence of iniquity.[30]

---

[30] In my next book on the topic of prayer I probe into the depth of what I call "Spiritual Intelligence" as it relates to achieving a God consciousness where Jesus' mandate to "be perfect" can be experienced at its highest level.

Being perfect is not a matter of whether one can achieve a level of always being sinless; it is about a nature and state of being that one can acquire through a required process that is coupled with fact that every human has the potential to *sin less* [1 John 3:6-9, 5:18]. The mandatory process is the removal of iniquity. This process heightens an awareness and nature that sets us free from any form of ungodly influences and from the contaminants of iniquity. The Kingdom of Heaven is holy and free of iniquity; its representatives that have the Kingdom of God within them on this earth—every member of the body of Christ—should manifest that same freedom.

> *"Then having these promises, dearly beloved, let us cleanse ourselves from all defilements of flesh and spirit, perfecting holiness in the fear of God"* (2 Cor. 7:1).

⌘

CHAPTER SUMMARY:

- Though we have access to the removal of iniquity through Jesus' death on the cross, many Christians still suffer from the effects of iniquity and its disastrous consequences.

- Though praying to accept Christ or going through the initial steps of being born again are good starts, they are not the complete cure for iniquity's presence and effects.

- Mercy and forgiveness do not remove iniquity completely; truth applied in the life of a believer is what permanently removes iniquity and its effects...as long as that truth is continually applied.

- Iniquity is also kept removed by the understanding and application of the fear of the Lord.

- Grace and truth cannot be separated. Grace is the portal for receiving truth. We received access to God's grace through Christ's death on the cross, yet we must not fail to seek after the Spirit of Truth for our lives.

- To be "saved" is to experience "the *vigor* of life." Vigor is the power of truth that is the "strength, energy or power to produce." Truth is this "power" that we are supposed to use in order to reproduce and create the works that we are saved to do that God has preordained for us.

- God prescribes truth for every aspect of our lives, even down to what we should eat and how we should physically take care of our bodies.

- Gluttony is rooted in iniquity; it is a sin that is being allowed to reign freely in the body of Christ, when believers should be the most disciplined group of people in the world today.

- When we take the time to listen to and record daily instructions from God, as He lets us know His will for our lives, this is the "scripture" for your personal life.

- A lifestyle of disciplined prayer and fasting paves the way to experiencing a preordained Kingdom of God life and relationship with God, free from any form of iniquity.

- Holiness *is not about* what we put on or take off physically; it's the very nature of God. To "be perfect" *is about* what we put on and take off mentally and spiritually; it's the very essence of what God is.

The Iniquity Removal Process

APPLICATION:

Following is a brief review of the iniquity-removal process.

1. Take the list that you made in the previous chapter and use it in your prayer life and as a blueprint to destroy iniquity in your life.

2. Ask God for forgiveness of any iniquity that you are guilty of, based off your internal inventory and your forefathers' iniquities.

3. Forgive your dad and forefathers of any hurt done to you and iniquity transferred to you.

4. Ask God for His prescription on how to root out and keep out any form of iniquity in your life, including any hereditary health issues. (Note: If you struggle with this or have never heard the voice of God, look for a resource to help you in this crucial process—whether it be a book on the subject of prayer or someone that can mentor you in how to hear the voice of God. Subscribe to my website for future teachings on prayer that includes updates on the release of my next book on the topic of prayer, which goes above and beyond traditional teaching of this crucial topic.)

5. Listen to what God says and document what He prescribes. (Remember that what God says to you is truth—original information that nurtures the covenant that He has with you and a law unto you to create order in your life.)

6. Take the steps He prescribes, coupled with strategic prayer and fasting.

7. Make a decision to no longer be negatively affected by the iniquity in your bloodline and commit to doing all that is necessary to root it out of your life.

8. Forgive yourself if you are carrying any guilt or shame due to something that you did to someone else or yourself due to the cancer of iniquity.

9. If you are led by God and it is wise and safe to do so, go and ask for forgiveness of those that you have hurt due to the iniquity in your life.

10. Remember that the removal and maintenance process of iniquity requires constantly taking an honest inventory of what is in your heart.

11. Practice hearing the voice of God daily, so that His truth will warn, instruct and uproot any form of iniquity in your life.

12. Remember to properly appropriate the blood of Jesus into your life, and to seek the washing of water that the Spirit of Truth provides.

CONCLUSION

We live in a fallen world, where iniquity has replaced purpose, sin has replaced righteous obedience, and vanity has replaced vigor.

It is not an exaggeration to state that iniquity has seeped into every family, every church, every nation and world government, and every single life in some way.

Our lives are meant to be lived with love, purpose, and Godly creativity; with joy, vision and holy righteousness; with peace, prosperity, and positive energy. All of these wonderful things come from the Spirit of God and He is waiting to pour them upon His children. It is not only so that we might have life more abundantly, although that is a great part of it; it is also that we might manifest Him and the truth of who He is to the entire world. We are meant to be the salt of the earth, the city on a hill, the light of the world.

God wishes for His children to shine as lights in the midst of the growing darkness of this world. Because of iniquity, however, instead of shining His light, so many Christians are instead sinking into the very darkness they are meant to pull others out of.

Jesus, when He was on earth, manifested the Name (identity, character and authority) of God—who He really was—to His disciples: "I have manifested thy name unto the men which thou gavest me out of the world: thine they were, and thou gavest them me; and they have kept thy word" (John 17:6, KJV). We hold that same truth and if we want to see the manifestations of God—His power and glory and exploits—we have to manifest His purpose and direction to the world.

Once again, iniquity is anything that turns one away from God's predestined, straight and perfect path for their lives. Iniquity is the root of all ignorance, darkness, sin and anything negative and unholy on this earth.

It was introduced to this world by Satan, the father of lies. And it continues to be birthed spiritually into the hearts and souls of people who choose not to rise above the evils of this world; it is also birthed biologically through fathers who have not claimed the power of the truth over their lives.

It all started with one man, Adam, and one fallen angel, Lucifer.

However, the power to overcome all evil and even the scourge of iniquity was also introduced through one Man, who walked and lived as a Man. He, the very Word of God "was made flesh and dwelt among us" so that we would be able to "behold His glory" and discover that He truly is "full of grace and truth" (John 1:14).

His grace through truth frees us to live the promise of a heavenly experience now on this earth and eternal life in Heaven. This includes the power to overcome the nature of fallen man here and now, and to be made anew as a child of God, recreated in His wonderful image.

God's truth cleanses us from sin and iniquity, and leads us in the path of righteousness. All we have to do is follow and allow our spirits to be cleansed with His blood, water and Spirit. His truth is the essence of God's love.

Today, just like in the Garden of Eden, there is *a tree of the knowledge of good and evil*. This tree contains the potential for iniquity. Many today are still eating from this tree, which is keeping them from eating from *the tree of life*. The "good" will often keep you from the "right." "There is a way which seems right to a man, but the end thereof is the way of death" (Prov. 14:12, 16:25). When one's life is filled with iniquity, it will make many things look "good." However, you must remember that evil is anything that doesn't line up with God's perfect will.

The Tree of Life is freely given to us; it is the tree of truth—Christ Jesus. His Words are spirit and they are life.

Now that you have completed this book, don't expect that your life will change in one day, or even a couple of weeks or months. However, within these pages, and within the pages of your Bible—if you truly study it with an open heart, and are honest with yourself and desperate for the Spirit of Truth to speak to your heart—you will begin to change.

God's Word will bring quickening (life) to your spirit. His Truth will bring cleansing to your soul. His Spirit will bring all good things into your heart and life, and in doing so, cast away all that is sinful and "iniquitized."

If every person, including those in religious settings and governmental and world leaders, would take the contents of this book and use it to root out iniquity from their lives and decision-making processes, much of the trouble that we see across the globe would slowly disappear and this world would truly become a better place to live.

It will be a process. It will most likely be a painful and challenging process, for you will need to open up your life to the direction of His Spirit and follow His leadings if you wish to truly leave iniquity in your past and embrace nothing but His grace and truth for your future.

You might find that your entire life is changing, and it might seem a little bit frightening. Change is never easy, so tell yourself that you are on the road to a life of wonders and miracles, as God begins to work in your life in ways you did not even think were possible.

"Old things are passed away; behold all things are become new" (2 Cor. 5:1).

"The people who know their God shall be strong and do exploits" (Dan. 11:32).

"They that be wise shall shine as the brightness of the firmament, and they that turn many to righteousness as the stars forever and ever" (Dan. 12:3).

Do you want to be made new? Do you want to be strong and do great exploits? Do you want to shine like the stars forever? Do you want to know and deploy the purpose for which God created you? Do you want to fix all that is wrong with you and discover all that is right about you? Do you want to discover God at level that just goes beyond mere knowledge of Him but have an intimate daily relationship with Him?

If the answer is yes to any of these questions, then do all that is necessary to root out the cancer of iniquity from your life. Then watch God do His part in showing you "The Real You" and "The Real Him" at the purest level. Follow God and His plan for your life and that is just what you will be anointed to do. You will become someone that you and the world have never known before, the person that you were supposed to have been all along ... all through the power of God and all for His glory.

Now that the mystery of iniquity has been revealed, I pray that your journey to eliminate all forms of iniquity will introduce you to the Vigor of God: The power (Truth) that God desires to deposit within the loins of your heart so that you can discover, develop and deploy "The Real You" in order to partner with "The Real God" in order to reproduce and create the works and life that have been predestined for you to do and live.

Amen.

⌘

ABOUT THE AUTHOR

Julio and his wife Ivette have been married for 19 years. In their blended family, they have three adult children and two grandchildren. Julio has been an employee at the Harley Davidson Motor Company for 22 years. Ivette is a licensed professional counselor with advanced clinical training in marriage and family therapy and sexual addiction.

Julio and Ivette attend World Outreach and Bible Training Center in Glendale, Wisconsin, serving under Pastors Ervin and Melva Henderson. They have served in a variety of ministries over the past 22 years, including the Pastoral/Leadership team, Men's Ministry, Discipleship Course Teachers, Youth and Children's Ministry, Small Group Facilitators, Home Bible Studies, and Lay Counseling. They have also ministered the Word of God to the corporate body.

In his life, Julio has overcome drug addiction, alcoholism, financial ruin, divorce, suicidal tendencies, depression and many other negative lifestyle issues. In February of 2006, after being a traditional Christian for over 15 years, Julio experienced a unique encounter with God. This experience birthed in him a hunger that changed the direction of his life. He began to pursue the truth about who God predestined him to be from a true "Kingdom of God" perspective. The vital discoveries Julio made have resulted in a complete about-face in his life, as well as the discovery of a new purpose: helping others discover who they really are in Christ. He follows God's original personal growth and development plan, which is to *Build One's Life from the Inside Out*.

Julio is currently starting a ministry which involves public speaking and teaching, creating books and other resources that transcend traditional religious teaching on key topics. These resources focus on rooting out iniquity from your life, learning how to hear the voice of God accurately and discovering your original preordained identity, purpose, vision, and mission for your life.

If you have questions or comments or would like to contact Julio and invite him to speak on the topic of this book as well as other life-changing topics you may contact him through his website at **www.julioalvaradojr.com** or email him directly at **julio@julioalvaradojr.com**

APPENDIX: DEFINITIONS

"Iniquity"

Strong's Concordance Definitions:

H5771 âvôn = perversity, that is, (moral) evil: - fault, mischief, punishment (of iniquity), sin

H5753 âvâh = do amiss, bow down, make crooked, bent, pervert, perverse, trouble, to turn, do wickedly, do wrong

H205 'âven = in vain; to come to naught); strictly nothingness; also trouble, vanity, wickedness; affliction, evil, false, idol, mischief, naught, sorrow, unjust, unrighteous, vain, wicked (-ness)

H5766 evel, âvel, avlâh, ôlâh = (moral) evil: perverseness, unjust (-ly), unrighteousness (-ly), wicked (-ness)

H2154 zimmâh, zammâh = a plan, especially a bad one: - heinous crime, lewd (-ly, -ness), mischief, purpose, thought, wicked (device, mind, -ness)

H2161 zâmam = to plan, usually in a bad sense: - consider, devise, imagine, plot, purpose, think (evil)

G458 anomia = illegality, that is, violation of law or (generally) wickedness: transgress (-ion of) the law, unrighteousness

G93 *adikia* = (legal) injustice (properly the quality, by implication the act); moral wrongfulness (of character, life or act): - unjust, unrighteousness, wrong

G3892 *paranomia* = See G3891; transgression: - iniquity

Brown-Driver-Briggs Hebrew Definition Dictionary:

H5771 âvôn = perversity, depravity, guilt or punishment

H5753 âvâh = to bend, twist, distort

H205 'âven = trouble, wickedness, sorrow

H5766 evel, âvel, avlâh, ôlâh = injustice, unrighteousness, wrong, violent deeds of injustice

H2154 zimmâh, zammâh = device, wickedness, evil plan, mischievous purpose

H2161 zâmam = to have an evil thought, devise, plan, consideration, purpose

Ancient Hebrew Lexicon of the Bible:

AHLB#:1512-(A-m)âvôn = Guilt: The result of twisted actions

AHLB#:1511-J(V)âvâh = Twist: To be twisted in ones actions. perverse, pervert, amiss, turn, crooked or bent, bow, trouble, wicked, wrong

AHLB#: 1014-J(N) = 'âven

Vigor: The power within the belly, or loins, for reproduction or creative work.

Appendix: Definitions

Vanity: The use of the power within the loins for vain or other improper purposes.

AHLB#: 1518-J(N) evel, âvel, avlâh, ôlâh, ôlâh = stained, wicked: unjust, unrighteous, perverse

AHLB#: 1151-A(N1) zimmâh, zammâh = Plot, Plan: The devising of a plan of action. Mischief: discretion, device, thought, wickedly, inventions, lewdness, mischievous

AHLB#: 1151-B (V) zâmam = Plot: To devise a plan of action,: thought, device, consider, purpose, imagination, plot usually with evil intent.

"Vanity"

Thayer Greek Dictionary:

G3153 mataiotēs = what is devoid of truth and appropriateness, perverseness, depravity, frailty, want of vigor

Greek to Hebrew Septuagint Dictionary:

G3153 mataiotēs To H7385 riq

Strong's Concordance:

H7385 *riq* = emptiness; figuratively a worthless thing, empty of contents, no purpose, (in) vain (thing), vanity

Ancient Hebrew Lexicon of the Bible:

riq AHLB#: 1456-M(N) = A container where all of its contents have been drawn out, empty of contents, no purpose.

"Without Form", "Void", "Darkness"

Strong's Concordance:

"Without form" =   H8414 tôhû = root meaning to lie waste; figuratively a worthless thing; adverbially in vain: - confusion, empty place, in vain, vanity, waste, wilderness.

"Void" =   H922 bôhû = root (meaning to be empty); an undistinguishable ruin: emptiness.

"Darkness" =   H2822 chôshek = the dark; figuratively misery, destruction, death, sorrow, wickedness. Ignorance (An absence of knowledge or revelation).

"Sin"

Strong's Concordance:

H2401 chăt͏̣âʼâh =   an offense

H2403 chat͏̣t͏̣âʼâh, chat͏̣t͏̣âʼth = an offense (sometimes habitual sinfulness), and its penalty, occasion, sacrifice, or expiation; also (concretely) an offender: - punishment (of sin)

H2398 chât͏̣âʼ =   A primitive root; properly to miss; by inference to forfeit, lack, expiate, repent, (causatively) lead astray, condemn: - bear the blame, by fault, harm done, loss

H817 ʼâshâm =   guilt; by implication a fault; guiltiness, (offering for) sin, trespass

H819 ʼashmâh =   guiltiness, a fault, the presentation of a sin offering: - offend, sin, (cause of) trespass (-ing, offering)

Appendix: Definitions

H2399 chêt.' =	a crime or its penalty: - fault, grievously, offense, (punishment of) sin
H6588 pesha =	a revolt (national, moral or religious): - rebellion, sin, transgression, trespassive
G266 hamartia =	sin (properly abstract): - offense, sin (-ful)
G264 hamartanō =	to miss the mark (and so not share in the prize), to err, especially (morally) to sin: - for your faults, offend, trespass

Brown-Driver-Briggs Hebrew Definition Dictionary:

H2401 =	chăt.â'âh = sin offering
H2403 =	chat.t.â'âh / chat.t.â'th = condition of sin, guilt of sin, punishment for sin, purification from sins of ceremonial uncleanness
H2398 =	chât.â' = miss, miss the way, go wrong, incur guilt, forfeit, purify from uncleanness, miss the goal or path of right and duty, to incur guilt, incur penalty by sin, forfeit, to bear loss, to miss the mark, to induce to sin, cause to sin, to bring into guilt or condemnation or punishment, to miss oneself, lose oneself, wander from the way.
H817 'âshâm =	guilt, offense, guiltiness, trespass, fault
H819 'ashmâh =	guiltiness, guilt, offense, doing wrong, committing a trespass or offense
H2399 chêt.'=	guilt for sin, punishment for sin
H6588 pesha'=	rebellion, transgression (against individuals), (nation against nation), (against God)

Ancient Hebrew Lexicon of the Bible:

AHLB#: 1170-E(N1) = A missing of the target. Also the sin offering which by transference becomes the sin.

AHLB#: 1170-E(N1) From H2403 = A missing of the target. Also a sinner as one who misses the mark. An offender, one with faults, acting grievously, one with offenses.

ALHB#: 1170-E(V) = The wrong actions of one are also measured against the correct action. To miss the target, whether a literal target or a goal that is aimed for.

AHLB#: 1473-C(N) = Guilt: One with a character of wrongdoing, trespass, guiltiness.

AHLB#: 1473-C(N1) = One with a character of wrongdoing. To trespass, to offend.

AHLB#: 1170-E(N) = When shooting an arrow or other object to a target, the distance that one misses is measured with a cord. The wrong actions of one are also measured against the correct action. A missing of the target. Also a sinner as one who misses the mark.

AHLB#: 2647(N) = Transgression, trespass, rebellion, to revolt. A spreading apart.

Thayer Greek Dictionary:

G264 hamartanō = To be without a share in, to miss the mark, to err, be mistaken, to miss or wander from the path of uprightness and honour, to do or go wrong, to wander from the law of God, violate God's law, sin.

Appendix: Definitions

G266 hamartia =	Equivalent to G264 with the additions of: That which is done wrong, sin, an offense, a violation of the divine law in thought or in act. Collectively, the complex or aggregate of sins committed either by a single person or by many.

"Grace"

Chen (Beauty)

AHLB#: 1175-A(N) =	A place of freedom.
AHLB#: 1175-H(V) =	To pitch a tent.
	Streams of water. [31]

---

[31] Jeff A. Benner. www.ancient-hebrew.org/12_thought.html Ancient Hebrew Research Center.

BIBLIOGRAPHY

Chapter Two:

James Strong, LL.D, S.T.D. *Strong's Concordance*. Thomas Nelson, 1st Ed. 1991.

Chapter Four:

Dr. Caroline Leaf: www.drleaf.com

Dr. Pepe Ramnath: www.mccint.org www.dovelabs.org

Chapter Nine:

"Worldwide Divorce Statistics." www.Divorce.com. 2012. Accessed 24 Mar. 2012.

Joseph Cardinal Mindszenty. Quote in *Life Before Life*. Author: Sarah Hinze.

Adler, B. Ronald and Russell F. Proctor. *Looking Out, Looking In*. 13th Edition. Cengage Learning. 2011.

"Children in Single-Parent Families." Data Across States. The Annie E. Casey Foundation. *Kids Count Data Center*. 2012. Accessed 24 Apr. 2012.

Chapter Ten:

"800 Million Go Hungry in Developing Nations." *Associated Press*. Deseret News. 14 Oct. 1994. 20 Mar. 2012.

Chapter Eleven:

Jeff A. Benner. "Ancient Hebrew Thought." www.ancient-hebrew.org. Ancient Hebrew Research Center. Accessed 20 Oct. 2012.

"John 7–IVP New Testament Commentaries." BibleGateway.com. Accessed 20 Oct. 2012. www.biblegateway.com/resources/commentaries/IVP-NT/John/Jesus-Source-Living-Water-All

Note: All Ancient Hebrew Lexicon of the Bible references (AHLB) come from The Ancient Hebrew Lexicon of the Bible by Jeff Benner: www.ancient-hebrew.org/bookstore /ahlb.html

www.ingramcontent.com/pod-product-compliance
Lightning Source LLC
Chambersburg PA
CBHW070556100426
42744CB00006B/297